YOU BE THE JUDGE

A Collection of Ethical Cases and Jewish Answers

Joel Lurie Grishaver

ISBN 978-1-961607-06-4

Published by Torah Aura Productions

TORAH AURA PRODUCTIONS • (800) BE-TORAH • (800) 238-6724 • (323) 585-7312
E-MAIL <MISRAD@TORAHAURA.COM> • VISIT THE TORAH AURA WEBSITE AT WWW.TORAHAURA.COM
MANUFACTURED IN USA

Prelude

The "Bet Din" process that has been captured in this book came to life as an accident in a family Torah class I was running at the University of Judaism. It was basically designed to be just a mixer—with a little learning attached. It surprised all of us as it quickly became something very powerful.

It started out with circles of families gathered around and serving as juries trying to solve difficult cases. It was fun and interesting to see them try to verbalize their values and their ethics as they struggled to apply them. It was powerful to see the way they grabbed at the pieces of Jewish learning they had at their disposal and twisted them into workable answers. The creativity and the conflict were inspiring.

A few have objected that I have polluted halakhah by letting the unlettered serve as legal decisors (and live with the fantasy that they can make decisions).

A few have objected that the exercise is folly—because religious law no longer has a place in a universe where every opinion is valid.

A few have objected that it was too Reform. Others that it was too Orthodox.

But the truth is, most of the time whether with kids, with families, with seniors—and then again among a broad-based electronic circle in first *Shabbas.Doc* and now *C.Ha*—the Sefat Emet has proved to be right:

> The entire Torah, God's teaching, was given to the Jewish people.
> Each person, however, has a personal Torah,
> a particular life goal that is concealed in the soul.
> When that particular teaching is released to the world
> the person moves toward the truth of his or her being.

GRIS

[1] The Kippah That Was Too Trustworthy

A full-time kippah-wearing Jew went to Texas to serve as an expert witness for the defense in a criminal trial. It was not a capital case. Before he could testify, the judge asked him to remove his kippah. He objected. He and the judge went into her chambers and exchanged words. He told the judge the meaning and the purpose of the kippah—that it showed that "God is always above me." The judge responded by telling him that the kippah gave him too much credibility. She was afraid that the jury would "over-trust" his testimony because of the fact that he was a religious man. He protested. She would not give in. If he tried to wear the kippah, he would be in contempt of court, sent to jail for several days, and would never be able to appear. The man called his rabbi to ask what he should do.

QUESTION: *If you were the rabbi, what would you tell the witness?*

The Answer to "The Kippah That Was Too Trustworthy"

Most authorities agree that nowhere in the Torah are men told to cover their heads. In the Talmud there are statements that some righteous men refused to walk more than six feet without covering their heads (*Shabbat* 118b and *Kiddushin* 29b). We also find these texts:

[a] Rabbi Nahman ben Isaac's mother was told by the astrologers before his birth that her son would grow up to be a thief. So she made sure that he was never bareheaded. She used to tell him, "Cover your head so that the fear of heaven will always be on you—and pray *for Divine help*." He did not know the reason why she did any of this. Then one day he was sitting and studying under a palm tree when the evil urge got the best of him. He climbed up the tree and stole a cluster of dates with his teeth. *After this he understood his mother's concerns* (*Shabbat* 156b).

[b] The Maharal (*Responsa Number* 7) makes it clear that a kippah is just a custom, a *minhag*. Any *minhag* that has been done by Israel for more than two hundred years is treated as if it is a rabbinic law.

[c] As to being a witness, the Torah says: "When a person is able to testify because s/he either saw or learned of a matter, and does not testify, s/he is subject to punishment" (Lev. 5.1).

[d] The *Shulhan Arukh* expands this and says: "It is a mitzvah to testify in court. In a criminal case (involving money, goods or possessions) one does not need to volunteer but must respond if summoned. In a capital case one must volunteer what one knows" (*Hoshen Mishpat* 25).

The witness's rabbi advised him that in Jewish law a biblical mitzvah takes precedence over a rabbinic mitzvah or a custom, so he should take off the kippah and testify. That is what he did.

[2] The Nolan Ryan Rookie Card Caper

The Atlas family owned a baseball card store and was awarded a free trip to the Super Bowl because of the number of cards they sold. They left a cousin to run the store. A Nolan Ryan rookie card is worth about $200. The cousin who was working in the card shop was a rookie, too, and knew little about card values. She misread the catalog (missing the asterisk that said "all prices times ten") when she quoted the kid $20. The kid was a baseball card shark. He knew a good deal when he heard one—even though he had just meant to "check out" the current value. He biked home, stole $20 from his mother's purse and then grabbed the card. The kid was also a regular. When the owner checked the day's sales and saw that this kid had bought that card for that price, he called him up and demanded that the deal be undone. The kid said, "A deal is a deal." The Atlas kid and the "shark" went to Hebrew school together. After the fight in the playground, the teacher took them to the principal, who told the rabbi, who called in the family for a conference. The rabbi held a Bet Din, a Jewish court.

BE THE JUDGE: *How do you resolve this case?*

The Answer to "The Nolan Ryan Rookie Card Caper"

In Jewish law there is a principle known as "a sale made in error." It is based on this Talmudic story:

Once there was a famine in a town named Nehardea. All the people had to sell their homes in order to afford to buy food to stay alive. When the wheat finally arrived and the famine ended, Rabbi Nahman made a ruling. He said, "Torah teaches that the houses must be returned to their original owners."

Rabbi Nahman's ruling needs explanation. The lack of food made the price of food rise. People sold their homes in desperation. What the people who sold their homes (the ones Rabbi Nahman made the purchasers return) didn't know was that the ship bringing food was already in the harbor, waiting for low tide to dock. The word had not yet gone out. But as soon as it did, the price of food would drop and everyone would be able to afford it without selling their homes. These sales were made without full information. They were based on an error in understanding. In Jewish law, any deal made with errors of understanding on either side can always be taken back.

And so the law follows Rabbi Nahman, ruling, "A person who sells a plot of land because s/he needed money, and after the sale learns that the money is not needed, can take the sale back" (*Ketubot 97a*).

That Talmudic text was taught to the two involved families, and they followed its recommendation.

[3] Nathan's Hundred Dollars

Nine-year-old Nathan, his little sister Becky and his mother are a family. Nine-year-old Nathan finds a hundred-dollar bill on the street. He walks home and says to his mother, "Look what I found." His mother says, "Perfect, now we will have no trouble paying this month's rent." Nathan says, "No way! It's mine." Mother says, "Wrong! As long as you live in my house and I work to pay the bills, I say where *our* money goes." The she added, "I'm sorry, though. If we could afford it, I would let you keep it." Nathan said, "I'm sorry, but you can't steal this from me." They fought and fought. Then Becky said, "No one should keep it. It belongs to someone else who lost it. If we can't find the owner, we should give it to tzedakah."

YOU ARE THE JUDGE: *Decide who is right.*

The Answer to "Nathan's Hundred Dollars"

Should nine-year-old Nathan keep the $100 he found?

[a] The first questions that must be asked are "Can anyone in the family keep the money? Do they have to try to return it?" Or, as Becky suggested, should they give it to tzedakah?

The Mishnah asks this very same question. It says:

"If one finds money in a purse…, a pile of money, or a stack of money…, one must try to find the owner" (*Bava Metzia* 2.2).

"If one finds scattered money, one may keep it" (*Bava Metzia* 2.1).

These two passages teach a basic idea called *hefker*. *Hefker* means "abandoned." The idea is this: once an owner would give up and no longer look for a lost object, then the finder might as well keep it. When one loses money (with no identification), one gives up very quickly; therefore the finder might as well not bother looking for the owner. If one finds something that can be identified, one must look for the owner. If one finds something that cannot be identified, one can just keep it.

In this case, the $100 bill can be kept. One need not look for the owner. One need not give it to charity.

[b] In the Gemara they ask this same question, and they say: "The finds of a child who is still supported by parents should be given to the parents for the sake of *darkhei shalom* (family peace)" (*Bava Metzia* 12a).

The idea is simple: As long as you are being supported by your parents, they are allowed to use the things you find or earn to help support the whole family, if necessary.

[c] However, in that same discussion the rabbis quote another discussion in a different part of the Talmud. There it says:

"It is forbidden to take a find away from a minor child who will not understand the reason why—and believe that his or her find was stolen away. This is for the sake of *darkhei shalom* (family peace). If you take it away, that child will learn that a bigger person is allowed to steal" (*Gittin* 5.8).

Therefore, if we follow Talmudic law, (1) the family may keep the hundred dollars, (2) Nathan should let his mother use the money for rent, but (3) she should not force him to do it if he can't understand the reasoning.

[4] The Burning Question of a Bike-a-thon on Shabbat

Randy is fifteen and an active member of her synagogue youth group. She also cares a lot about the world. She is one of those people who are involved and who volunteer for every good cause. She is a good kid. The problem started with a bike-a-thon for hunger. It was a big citywide event that was scheduled for a Saturday (because the sponsoring churches didn't want it on Sunday.) Randy wanted the youth group to bike to help the homeless. The powers-that-be in the synagogue said "Not on Shabbat." Randy was angry; she and a group of her friends decided to go anyway. Her parents said no. They said, "The Torah says that Jews should keep Shabbat." Randy said, "Sure, but it also teaches you to help those who are hungry and homeless."

YOU GET TO DECIDE: *Who is right? What should Randy do about the Shabbat bike-a-thon?*

The Answer to "The Burning Question of a Bike-a-thon on Shabbat"

This case asks: "Can you do 'work' on Shabbat if it is for a mitzvah?"

[a] In the book of Exodus we learn that it is a mitzvah (commandment) not to work on Shabbat: "Six days you shall labor, doing all your work; but the seventh day is Shabbat to the Eternal, your God. On it you shall not do any work, not you, not your son, not your daughter, not your manservant, or your maidservant, or your cattle, and not even the visitor who is staying with you" (Exodus 20.9-10).

[b] In the Talmud they define "work" as doing any one of the thirty-nine things that were needed to build the *mishkan* (tabernacle). Our bike-a-thon requires "work" in two or three ways: (1) Earning money, even for a good cause, is considered work. (2) Moving objects from place to place is considered work. In this case, the bikers are moving the bicycles. (3) There is a limit on how far you can travel on Shabbat. The route (unless it is a lot of laps of a very small circle) will violate that, too.

[c] In the Talmud we learn a principle called *pikuah̲ nefesh*. It teaches that the Shabbat can be broken to save a human life. It comes from this story:

Hillel the Elder was very poor. He used to work and earn only two small coins a day. Half of the money he would give to the guard at the door to the yeshivah; the other coin would be spent for his food and for that of his family. One day he earned nothing, and the guard would not let him enter. He climbed up and sat upon the window to hear the lesson. That day was the eve of Sabbath on the shortest day of the year, and snow fell down upon him from heaven.

The next morning Shemayah said to Abtalion: "Brother Abtalion, every day this house is light, but today it is dark. Maybe it is a very cloudy day." They looked up and saw the figure of a man in the window. They went up and found Hillel covered by three cubits of snow. They removed him and lighted a fire. They bathed and anointed Hillel and placed him opposite the fire. They said: "Better we should violate this Shabbat so that he can celebrate many Shabbatot in the future" (*Yoma 35b*).

[d] In the Mishnah we find this rule about breaking Shabbat to do a mitzvah:

A building collapses. It is possible that a person is lost in the rubble under it. But it is also possible that no one is under the rubble. It is possible that if there is a victim, the victim is alive, and it is possible that the victim is not alive. You must dig for survivors through the heap of debris **even on Shabbat.**

If they find her/him alive, they must remove the debris but if they find him/her dead, they must stop until after Shabbat (*Mishnah, Yoma* 8.7).

[e] The Talmud teaches:

"There are two ways for a rich person inside a house to give something to a poor man outside the house. One way violates Shabbat. The other way doesn't" (*Shabbat* 1.1).

From this we learn that there are ways of helping the poor and keeping Shabbat. The Talmud suggests that Randy and her friends look for ways to both help the homeless and observe Shabbat, rather than setting it up as a choice.

[5] The Ethics of Change

Hillary goes to the grocery store and buys $7.75 worth of groceries. She gives the cashier a ten-dollar bill and receives what she thinks is $2.25 in change. Outside in the parking lot Hillary notices that instead of two single dollars and a quarter, the cashier mistakenly gave her a ten-dollar bill and a one. She has gotten $11.25 change and made money on the purchase. She starts to walk away. One voice in her head says, "The cashier made the mistake. I am just reaping the reward." The other voice in her head says, "Walking away is like stealing."

YOUR TURN: *What should she do?*

The Answer to "The Ethics of Change"

Hillary goes to the grocery store and gets $11.25 change when she deserves $2.25. Must she return the difference?

[a] We know that stealing is against the Torah. It is one of the commandments:

YOU SHALL NOT STEAL (Exodus 20.13).

It is also mentioned in the Holiness Code, where it says:

"You shall not steal, and you shall not deceive, and you shall not lie to one another. You should not use My name to lie, profaning the name of your God. I am the Eternal" (Leviticus 19.11-13).

Rashi points out that God connected all of these laws together to show that anyone who steals (or lies or deceives) denies that there is One God who is the parent of all people.

[b] The rabbis said that no matter how small the theft, it is still a theft. They told this story to explain:

"In Noah's time, when someone took a bushel of beans to sell in the marketplace, another person would just walk by and grab less then a penny's worth of beans to munch on. The muncher didn't worry about it, because all he took was a couple of beans. Then another person would do the same thing. And then another. Soon the bushel was empty. There was nothing left to sell! There was also no one to take to court to make pay. This was the evil that God saw when deciding on the flood" (*Genesis Rabbah* 30).

[c] Summarizing Talmudic law in *The Jewish Encyclopedia of Moral and Ethical Issues*, Norman Amsel explains:

"It could be argued that this teenager did nothing wrong and didn't ask for the money; therefore it is not stealing. That, however, is wrong. Knowing that the extra change will come out of the cashier's salary or out of the owner's profit, it would be stealing from the moment she realized she had the extra money and walked away."

[6] The Case of Barney's Rubble

Fred had hundreds and hundreds of shot glasses. Every time he went on a trip he bought a shot glass. Soon his house was filled with them. After a while he put them in boxes. Then he moved to a smaller apartment with no storage space. Fred didn't know what to do with the glasses. He decided to leave them in his friend Barney's garage until he figured out where to put them. He knocked on Barney's door. There was no answer. Fred put them on a shelf in Barney's unlocked garage anyway. A week later, fifteen-and-half-year-old Elroy, working on his learner's permit, drives the car too far into the garage, hits the shelf and knocks the boxes onto the floor and onto the car. Fred wants Barney to pay to replace the broken glasses. Barney wants Fred to pay to repair the flat tire the broken glass caused.

YOU BE THE JUDGE: *Decide who is right.*

The Answer to "The Case of Barney's Rubble"

Fred leaves his "junk" in Barney's garage without telling anyone. Elroy, Fred's son, destroys them by accident. Who is responsible?

This case is straight out of the Mishnah. In *Bava Metzia* 5.2 we find:

"If a potter leaves his pots in the courtyard of another and the owner's cattle breaks them,

[a] If s/he had no permission to leave them, then (1) the owner of the cattle has no obligation to pay for them, and (2) the potter must pay if the pots injured the cattle.

[b] If s/he had permission to leave them, then (1) the owner of the cattle must pay for them, and (2) the potter has no obligation to pay if the cattle are injured.

Based directly on this mishnah, Fred must pay for the tire and is not repaid for the glasses.

[7] Who Gets Grandma's Loot?

One evening Grandma came over to show her new will to her daughter. She had worked hard at it with her lawyer. She was very proud. She told her daughter, "I've managed to give it all away to good causes." Her daughter swallowed once and then asked, "You've given it all away to causes?" Grandma said, "You bet—that money is going to do a lot of mitzvot." Her daughter swallowed again and asked, "You mean you've left nothing for me and nothing for my children?" Grandma answered, "You've got a great job, and your family has more than everything they need. You've done well. And I don't want my grandchildren thinking that they don't have to earn their own way. The best gift I can give them is my example in being socially responsible." Now, almost losing her temper, the daughter said, "But providing for your family is a mitzvah, too. You can give a lot of money away, but you should leave something for us as well." The argument continued and did not reach an end.

YOUR TURN: Decide who is right. Should Grandma change her will?

The Answer to "Who Gets Grandma's Loot"

This case was adapted from a chapter in *How Does Jewish Law Work?* by J. Simcha Cohen, Jason Aronson, 1986. The question: Can Grandma leave all her money to good causes and none to her family?

[a] Rabbi Barukh ha-Levi Epstein, the scholar who wrote the *Torat Temimah*, said, "There is no Jewish obligation to leave one's children an inheritance." He based his opinion on this midrash:

Rabbi Meir earned three coins a week. One went for his food. One went for his clothing. And one was given as tzedakah. When students asked, "Don't you have to leave an inheritance for your children?" he said no and quoted Psalm 37, "I HAVE NEVER SEEN A RIGHTEOUS PERSON GO HUNGRY."

[b] In *Ketubot* 50 the Talmud says that one should limit one's tzedakah to twenty percent of one's income and not cause one's family distress. The Talmud says:

"Rabbi Elai stated, 'It was ordained at Usha that if a person wishes to spend liberally on giving *tzedakah* s/he should not spend more than a fifth of his/her wealth, because if one did, one might ultimately need to receive *tzedakah*.'"

This text does not mandate leaving an inheritance but does seem to set a limit on charitable giving.

[c] There is no clear Talmudic answer to this one, so Grandma probably cannot be stopped by halakhah. But she can probably be encouraged not to exclude her family.

[8] Mishnah Goes to the Movies—*The War*

The movie *The War* with Kevin Costner and Elijah Wood echoes a famous Talmudic case. In the movie the Costner character is in Vietnam and carries a wounded friend for miles to save his life. When he is rescued by the helicopter he finds out that there is room for only one on this helicopter (it cannot lift any more weight). And he finds out that this is the last helicopter. He must choose between saving himself and saving his very badly wounded and fairly-certain-to-die friend. (In the Talmud, we have a case where two men are in the desert and only one has a canteen. If they share, both will die.)

FIGURE IT OUT: *What should Costner do?*

The Answer to "Mishnah Goes to the Movies—"

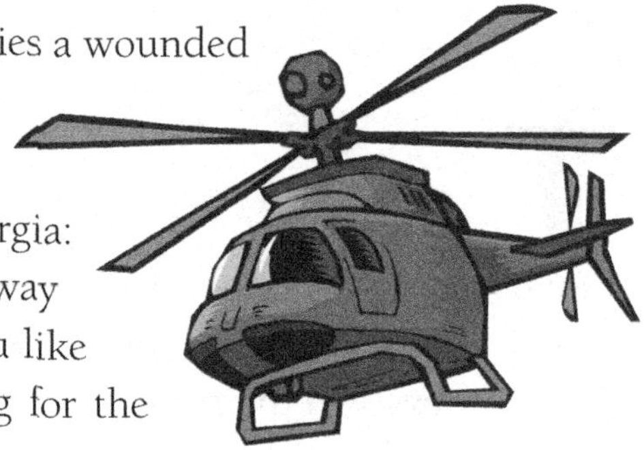

In the movie *The War,* the Costner character is in Vietnam and carries a wounded friend for miles to save his life, then finds out that there is room for only one on the helicopter. What should Costner do?

[a] Our friends the Fishman family wrote from Augusta, Georgia: "We enjoyed discussing this case. Steven says that the way you would do it in Special Forces is to throw out the guy that you like the least. I'm not sure that I agree with that. We are all waiting for the answer."

[b] In the Talmud, *Bava Metzia 62a*, we find this case:

"Two people are traveling on a journey far from civilization. One of them has a pitcher of water. If they share the water, they will both die, but if one only drinks, he can reach civilization. What should they do?"

"The Son of Patura taught: It is better that both should drink and die, rather than that one should behold his companion's death. "

R. Akiba won the argument by quoting Leviticus 25.36 where it says:

"If your brother/sister becomes poor and near you—his hand falters—you shall hold onto him—either Jew-by-choice or citizen—so that s/he can live *with you.*"

Rabbi Akiva emphased the words "with you." He said that they established a principle that we don't reject one life to save another. Therefore, you don't share the water when both of you will die—you drink it yourself.

[c] Sifra on Leviticus 25.36 says: "You do not judge 'whose blood is redder.' You save yourself".

Talmudically, Costner does the right thing—despite the guilty feelings—when he gets on the plane and saves himself.

[9] Can You Cheat at Torah?

Robert got caught cheating on a Torah test at his day school. The principal told him that he was going to be suspended for cheating and might be expelled. Robert said, "Where in the Torah does it say that cheating is a sin? What law does it break? Besides, if you kick me out of school, I am going to learn even less Torah, and I do know that teaching me is a mitzvah. It says in the Torah, 'AND YOU SHALL TEACH THEM TO YOUR CHILDREN' (Deuteronomy 6.7). It seems to me that my reviewing my Torah facts on a crib sheet was a way of learning more Torah—while your kicking me out of school is breaking the Torah." Then he folded his hands and smiled.

YOUR TURN: *Imagine what you would tell Robert after the principal called and told you this story. Also—is cheating on a Torah exam against the Torah?*

The Answer to "Can You Cheat at Torah?"

Robert cheats on a Torah exam and then says that cheating on Torah is not against the Torah.

[a] In a *t'shuvah* (a responsum), Rabbi Menasheh Klein says that cheating on any exam (Torah or secular) is prohibited as *g'nevat da'at*, "stealing a mind." It is a kind of fraud and a violation of one of the Ten Commandments, "YOU SHALL NOT STEAL" (Exodus 20. 13). This is because you have stolen the truth and replaced it with a false impression. Cheating at an exam also makes each of your classmates less. They may not get into as good a school or get as good a job.

[b] When it comes to cheating at Torah, Rambam (Maimonides) says it is a double sin—and adds *hillul ha-Shem* (embarrassing God) to *g'nevat da'at* (mind stealing) (*Mishneh Torah*, *Laws of Faith*, 6). The idea that anyone could study Torah and then be dishonest says that the Author (God) had no impact.

[c] Finally, it is good for parents and teacher to "correct" Robert and "help him reconsider" because the Torah makes it a mitzvah to "reprove" a fellow Jew: YOU MUST TELL YOUR PEOPLE WHEN THEY ARE DOING WRONG (Leviticus 19.17).

[10] Hanukkah Overkill

Deborah's Hebrew school teacher made a big deal out of teaching the class that the big mitzvah of Hanukkah is to "advertise the miracle." She said that the real idea was to let everyone see your hanukkiyah and to tell the story of Hanukkah to as many people as possible. Deborah told this to her parents, and she and her father spent the next week working in the garage making a huge oil-burning hanukkiyah. When Hanukkah came they put it on the front lawn. The hanukkiyah was so large that lights six, seven and eight stuck out into the street. On the last night of Hanukkah Zvi was walking past Deborah's house to a Hanukkah party, carrying a whole bunch of balloons. At just the wrong moment the wind picked up and blew the balloons into light eight, and they exploded and went up in flames. The wind took the burning ribbon and plastic and blew it into Fido's doghouse, which burned down. Of course, there was a big fight over who should rebuild the dog house—Deborah or Zvi.

COURT TIME: *Decide who is responsible. Is this negligence or an act of God?*

The Answer to "Hanukkah Overkill"

Who is responsible for the party balloons that caught fire from the oversized hanukkiyah in Deborah's front yard? There is a Mishnah that specifically addresses this problem.

[a] In *Bava Kamma* 6:6 we find:

"If a camel was loaded with flax and was walking on a public street, and some of the flax stuck into a shop and caught fire on the storekeeper's lamp, and in turn the building caught fire, the camel owner would be responsible. If the lamp was outside the store, then the store owner must pay. But if the lamp was a hanukkiyah, the camel owner must pay."

Therefore Zvi is responsible for what his flaming balloons did, even though the hanukkiyah was sticking out into the street. If it had been any other kind of fire, Deborah's family would have to pay.

[b] The Talmud made an exception for hanukkiyot because of the rule:

"The mitzvah of Hanukkah is to advertise the Miracle" (*Shabbat* 21b).

There are two notions: (a) That on Hanukkah one should have an expectation of public hanukkiyot and therefore be careful. And (b) that rather than make people fearful of showing off their hanukkiyot and doing Hanukkah in a big way, hanukkiyot are given a liability exception. This is a unique and special Hanukkah law.

[12] Family Feud

Danny is eight. His best friend, Robbie, is also eight. They do everything together. Their fathers used to be best friends, too. The problem started when Danny's father borrowed a lawn mower from Robbie's father. The next time Robbie's father went to use that lawn mower for his lawn it was broken. He blamed Danny's dad. Danny's dad said, "It worked fine when I returned it." The lawn mower was the start of the big fight. Things got worse and worse. It made it harder and harder for Danny and Robbie to hang out together. Then one day Danny's father said to him, "I don't want you playing with Robbie anymore—and I want you to listen to me, because I am your father." Danny asked his rabbi the following question: "I know that the Torah says 'Honor your father and mother,' but do I have to honor him when he's being stupid?"

TIME TO DECIDE: *Work out an answer to Danny's question.*

The Answer to "Family Feud"

Can Robbie's and Danny's fathers stop them from being best friends?

[a] One of the 613 mitzvot is Leviticus 19.17:

"Do not hate your brother/sister in your heart."

Some commentators explain that brother/sister means another Jew; others say that it means any other person. Therefore, Danny's father's attitude and behavior are against the Torah.

[b] Rabbi Asher Ben Yechiel, who was known as the Rosh, lived in Toledo, Spain, in the early 1300s and actually had to solve a case like this. He started with Rashi's comment on Leviticus 19.2. The verse says:

"(1) Every person must "fear" his/her mother and father, (2) and all of you shall keep my Shabbatot, (3) I am the Eternal, Your God."

RASHI: "Why are all three parts of the verse packed into one sentence? To teach this lesson. That (1) you must 'obey' your parents unless they tell you (2) that you must violate the Shabbat or break any other Torah commandment, because (3) I am the Eternal, and I am God to them and God to you. Parental authority is absolute unless they tell you to go against the Torah. God is the final word."

[c] The Rosh said, "By giving such an order the father was acting in an un-Jewish manner. This being so, the son need not obey him."

[13] The Magic That Fails

Rob had over five hundred Magic cards. He loved to collect them. And playing Magic was his third favorite thing to do in the whole world. One summer afternoon Rob and Corey were playing Magic on the picnic table in Rob's backyard. Rob's mother interrupted the game to send Rob on an errand to the store. Rob did a chorus of "But, Mom, we're playing." It did no good. He went off to the store. Corey went home to clean his room (something that had to be done before his mother got home). The two piles of Magic cards were left on the picnic table under ten-pound weights from the weight set in the backyard so they wouldn't blow away. Then tragedy struck. Rain came down. Rob was at the store. Corey was collecting dirty underwear from all over his basement room. Rob's mother sent Rob's sister Janet outside to rescue the cards. That is where the fight started. She got Rob's cards but left Corey's sitting under the weight on the picnic table in the rain. She claimed she wasn't responsible for Corey's things.

NOW DECIDE THIS ONE: *Was Janet right? Did she have a choice whether or not to save Corey's cards?*

The Answer to "The Magic That Fails"

Rob's sister left Corey's Magic cards out in the rain while she recued her brother's deck.

[a] In the Torah we find this verse:

"If you see your neighbor's ox or sheep lost, you must not ignore it… You must do the same thing for anything that is your neighbor's—you must not remain indifferent" (Deuteronomy 21:1-3).

[b] In the Talmud, *Bava Metzia* 30b, the idea is expanded.

"If a person sees flood waters approaching someone else's field, that person must make a barrier or a dam and try to stop them in order to prevent damage to the neighbor's property."

Therefore we learn that Janet was wrong. One cannot stand by and watch someone else's property be destroyed.

[14] The Shabbat Picnic

On a hot August night the Kaufman family decided to have their Shabbat dinner as a picnic on the porch instead of in the dining room. Instead of a white embroidered tablecloth, it was going to be a plastic red checked tablecloth. Instead of the good china it was going to be paper plates. Mom was all excited. She wasn't going to have to do any dishes at all. It was a great Shabbat present. She even went to the store and bought two red glass table candles with plastic mesh (like you find in a pizza palors) to be the Shabbat candles. When the family sat down to eat Dad and Mom had a halakhic discussion. (It wasn't a fight.) Dad looked at the paper cup that Mom had set next to the bottle of wine as a "picnic kiddush cup" and said, "This is wrong. Kiddush should be made from a good cup because it is a mitzvah." Mom said, "It is the blessing and feeling that matters." Then everyone at the table gave an opinion.

WHAT IS YOUR VOTE: *Give your opinion.*

The Answer to "The Shabbat Picnic"

There is a Jewish value known as *hiddur mitzvah*. It is the commitment to make every mitzvah as beautiful as possible.

[a] In the midrash we are taught:

"What is the meaning of the verse, THIS IS MY GOD—I HONOR HIM (Genesis 15.2)? How can a person who is only flesh and blood honor the Creator? Easy! We do it by performing the commandments in as beautiful and honorable a way as possible. For God I will have a beautiful lulav, a beautiful shofar on Rosh ha-Shanah, a beautiful tallit, a beautiful Torah scroll written with total dedication by a qualified scribe with a quality quill and fine ink and wrapped in the purest silk.

Based on this principle, kiddush cups, too, are supposed to be beautiful.

[b] In 1968 Rabbi Moshe Feinstein answered this question for Mr. Aryeh Leib Bobbins. He said, "The Tosefot comment on *Brakhot* 50 in the Talmud that a kiddush cup should be in perfect condition. Thus we are required to use a graceful cup." He concludes that a disposable paper cup is not desirable but may be used if there is no other choice.

[c] It is unclear how any of these texts apply to the question of a Shabbat picnic. What do you think?

[15] Behavioral Change

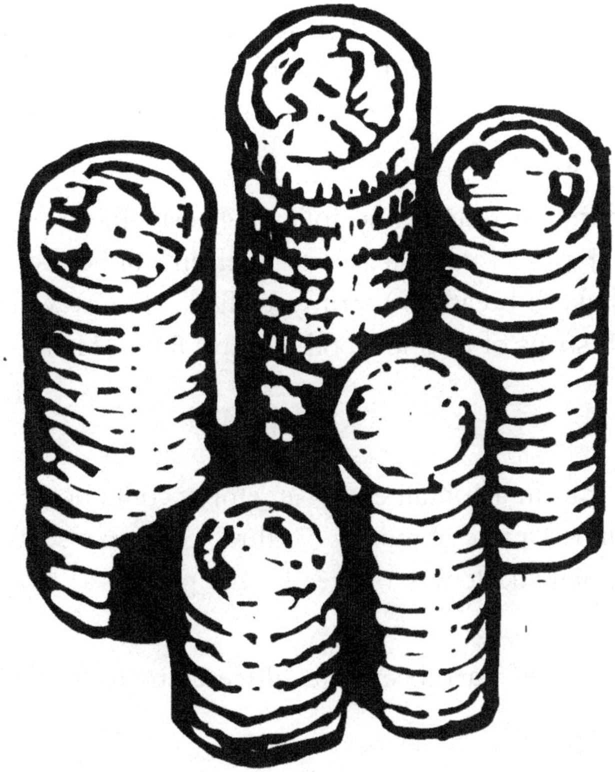

Jody is one of those kids who walk down the street phone booth by phone booth. At every phone booth she stops and checks for change. Every now and then she picks up an odd dime or quarter this way. One day she walks by a phone, finds more than two dollars in change and yells for joy. She starts to scoop out the money. All of a sudden a woman with a camera around her neck screams from the other side of the street, "Stop, that's my money!" Jody says, "No way. It was sitting right there in a public phone. and I found it. Your name wasn't on it." The woman said, "I was on the phone and saw the blue-breasted robin I had been hunting for. I hung up with my mother and went to take the picture. Now I am on the way back to get the change." Jody said, "If that's the case, tell me how much money there is." The woman said, "I don't know. I put in eight dollars in quarters and started to talk. I don't know how much change the phone gave me, but it's mine." The argument went on for a while.

YOU BE THE JUDGE: *Decide who should get the money.*

The Answer to "Behavioral Change"

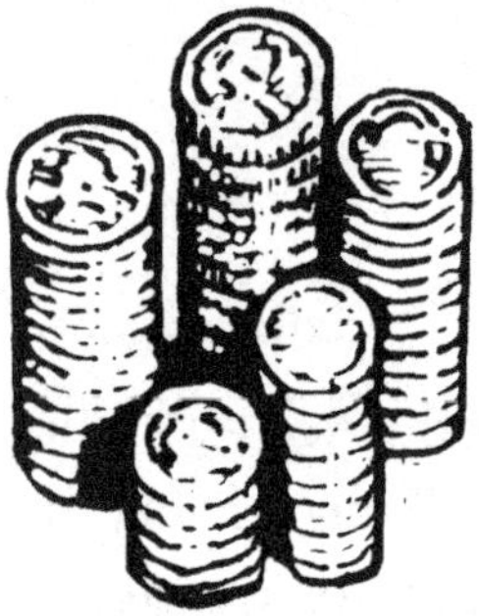

The Mishnah gives us very clear ground rules for when we can keep something we find and when we need to try to return it to the person who lost it.

[a] In *Bava Metzia* 2.1 we are told:

One may just keep (without trying to return) the following lost objects: (1) scattered fruit, (2) scattered money, (3) small sheaves of grain in public areas, (4) cakes of figs, (5) loaves of baker's bread, (6) strings of fish, (7) raw wool shearings, (8) bundles of flax, (9) strips of purple wood. So says Rabbi Meir."

[b] In *Bava Metzia* 2.2 we are told:

"One must try to return the following lost objects: (1) fruit in a container, (2) an empty container, (3) money in a purse, (4) an empty purse, (5) a pile of fruit, (6) a pile of money, (7) three coins in a stack, (8) small sheaves of grain on private property, (9) homemade loaves of bread, (10) processed wool shearings, (11) jars of oil or wine.

Had the woman known the amount of the change, it would have been like "three coins in a pile." Because she didn't, it is like "scattered coins."

[c] In *Bava Metzia* 2.1 we are given the basic principle.

"Rabbi Judah says: 'Everything unusual must be advertised.'"

Based on the Mishnah, because the coins could not be identified, Jody may keep the money. Though that may not be fairest thing, it is the most practical solution. However, if the woman can describe anything about the coins, Jody must give them to her.

[16] The Bogus Well-Meaning Pledge

It was a scam—but it was for a good purpose. It happened at a synagogue meeting. Sara was the chairperson. The purpose was to raise money for a new school building. The idea was to get everyone to fill out a pledge on a card. To get the ball rolling Dana, Sidney and Marcia, a few of the synagogue's leaders, stood up and announced their personal pledges. They were large and impressive. Then the pledge cards and pencils were passed out. Later that night, when David, the synagogue treasurer, was going over the cards, he noticed that the actual pledges by Dana, Sidney and Marcia were less than half of what they had announced publicly. He went to Sara and asked, "What should we do?" Sara said, "Nothing. That was the plan, to announce large pledges to 'get the ball rolling'—to encourage the others in the congregation to give freely." David said, "A false pledge is unethical—we should go to the congregation and tell them the truth." Sara said, "Cool your jets—it was all in the name of Jewish education."

TIME FOR JUDMENT: *What should be done about these bogus pledges?*

The Answer to "The Bogus Well-Meaning Pledge"

Can you lie in order to raise more money for a good cause?

[a] In the Talmud, *Sukkot* 29a, we find:

"God causes people to lose their wealth because of four acts: (1) keeping bills which have been paid (so they can be collected again); (2) lending money with interest; (3) having the power to protest [*against wrongdoing*] and remaining silent; and (4) people who publicly declare their intention to give a specified sum for charity and do not give that sum."

The Talmud says that "God will punish such acts, even if they are done for a good purpose."

[b] The Maharasha, Rabbi Shmuel ha-Levi Eidels (1555-1631), was the rabbi of Chelm (for real, as well as of Lublin and Ostraha). He was also a Talmudic commentator. He explained that this ruling in *Sukkot* is not just about people who make large pledges so that they will look important, but also about active members of the community who make large pledges they have no intention paying, but who do so just to motivate others to give.

[c] Rabbi Yitzhak Yaakov Weiss, a twentieth-century rabbi who served as a Bet Din judge in Grosswardein, Romania, Manchester, England, and Jerusalem, solved a case almost just like this one. It is in his book *Minhat Yitzhak* (no. 3:97), where he says, "This has been a custom since time immemorial, and our sages have always frowned on it, including making it among the four failings for which a severe punishment is exacted."

MORE TO THINK ABOUT: *What do you think the congregation should do at this point?*

[17] Model Behavior

It is Sunday afternoon, and Bob is working on a new plastic model kit of one of the star cruisers from *Star Wars.* In the middle of the work he runs out of cement. He tears his room apart and finds that this was his last tube. He gets on his bike and rides to Geoff's house. Geoff has a whole box of tubes. Geoff says to Bob, "Because I like you, I'll do you a favor. I'll sell you a $1.79 tube for $5. Otherwise, you can wait until the model shop opens again on Monday." Bob says, "It's robbery, but I'll pay it." He takes the tube and finishes the model. Later, his older brother tells him it was robbery. The two of them go and demand that Geoff return $3. Geoff says, "You knew what I was doing. You agreed. A deal is a deal."

BE THE JUDGE: *Decide who is right.*

The Answer to "Model Behavior"

Geoff overcharged Bob for a tube of glue he really wanted. Now Bob wants Geoff to refund the overcharge.

[a] In the Talmud there is a category called *ona'ah moneh* that covers overcharging. There are two basic rules: (1) You cannot charge more than twenty percent of the "regular" price of something without telling the buyer about the overcharge. (2) You can never charge more than twenty percent over the usual price of basic necessities (bread, eggs, milk, grain, etc.) (*Bava Metzia* 49b).

So normally Geoff would be able to keep the profit, because he made the price difference clear to Bob.

[b] *Bava Kamma* 115a tells the story of a guy who was escaping from Roman soldiers and so agreed to pay a ferry pilot three times the normal price to take him over the river in order to escape. Later the rabbis made the ferry pilot return the excess fare (because he was taking advantage of the situation).

[c] Rabbi Joel Sirkes (1561-1640) applied that text to the case of a businessman who intentionally paid too much for goods in order to complete a shipment. Later he, too, took the matter to court and got everything past a twenty percent extra profit back—even though he had agreed to the price at the time.

He got his money back, and so should Bob.

[18]: The Misgivings of a Torah Cover

It was a very tricky question. In honor of Deborah's bat mitzvah, her Grandmother Ruth wanted to donate a new Torah cover she had sewn to the congregation. It was really beautiful. The problem was that Grandmother Ruth, who was born a Jew, converted to Christianity to marry her second husband, Frank, long after Deborah's mother Pam was already an adult. The congregation had to decide two things: (1) Is it okay to dress the Torah in a gift given by a non-Jew? (2) Is there a difference between a gift given by a non-Jew and a gift given by a Jew who is now actively practicing another religion?

SOLVE THIS ONE: *Give your answer to these two questions.*

The Answer to "The Misgivings of a Torah Cover"

Sometime around 1460 Rabbi Yisrael Brunna solved a similar case in Prague. He teaches two lessons:

[a] The Talmud says that the Temple in Jerusalem (*Nazir* 62a) accepted pledges and free-will offerings from non-Jews. Our synagogues should do the same.

[b] The Talmud states that we do not accept gifts to the Temple from Jews who have converted to another religion (*Eruvin* 69b).

[c] While Rabbi Brunna uses this passage to reject the gift from the Christian grandmother, that may not be the only reading.

In a similar Reform responsa Walter Jacobs points out that the gifts for the Temple mentioned in *Eruvin* were connected to idolatry. Here we may see Christians not as pagans, but as ethical monotheists. He writes: "Such gifts are acceptable as long as they are used in accordance with the desires of the congregation."

[19] Is Hate a Sin?

Jimmy lived across the street from David. Jimmy always picked on David. He called him names. He threw things at him. He stepped on the backs of his shoes. He pushed ahead of him in line. He knocked his books off his desk. He got his friends to do the same thing.

At dinner David's parents announced that on Sunday afternoon Jimmy's family was coming over for a barbecue. David said, "No way." His parents asked why. He said, "I hate him." He went through all the things that had happened. His father said, "It is good that they are coming over. That way you can tell him how you feel." David said, "No way. I just hate him." His father said, "Hating someone is a sin. What we need to do is work on the way Jimmy acts." David said, "My feelings are my feelings. A feeling can't be a sin. I hate him."

BE THE JUDGE: *Decide who is right this time.*

The Answer to "Is Hate a Sin?"

Can a feeling (hate) be against Jewish law?

[a] The last of the ten commandments is:

YOU SHALL NOT COVET YOUR NEIGHBOR'S HOUSE, YOU SHALL NOT COVET YOUR NEIGHBOR'S WIFE, NOR HIS MANSERVANT, NOR HIS MAIDSERVANT, NOR HIS OX, NOR HIS ASS, NOR ANY THING THAT IS YOUR NEIGHBOR'S (Exodus 20.14).

[b] Ibn Ezra, a medieval biblical commentator, writes:

"There are three kinds of mitzvot: mitzvot of the heart, mitzvot of the tongue and mitvot of action. Those of the heart can be divided into 'do-mitzvot' and 'don't-mitzvot.' Heart mitzvot are about feelings.

Some 'do-mitzvot' are: 'Love the Eternal your God' (Deut. 6.5) and 'Love your neighbor as yourself' (Lev. 19.18).

Some 'don't mitzvot' are: 'Do not hate your brother/sister in your heart' (Lev. 17: 17) and 'Do not bear a grudge'" (Lev. 17: 18).

[c] Maimonides disagrees with him and believes that "COVET" requires an action. He bases this on the repetition of the Ten Commandments in Deuteronomy, where it says:

YOU SHALL NOT DESIRE YOUR NEIGHBOR'S WIFE. YOU SHALL NOT COVET YOUR NEIGHBOR'S HOUSE, HIS FIELD, OR HIS MANSERVANT, OR HIS MAIDSERVANT, HIS OX, OR HIS ASS, OR ANY THING THAT IS YOUR NEIGHBOR'S (5.18).

Maimonides explains:

"When one schemes to acquire some property that belongs to a neighbor, one has violated the command, 'YOU SHALL NOT DESIRE ANYTHING THAT BELONGS TO YOUR NEIGHBOR' (Law 10). When one puts pressure on one's neighbor to part with property (against his/her will) one has violated the command: 'YOU SHALL NOT COVET' (Law 9). Desire leads to coveting, and coveting leads to robbery" (Law 11). *The Book of Mitzvot.*

For Ibn Ezra, thoughts can be sins. For Maimonides, actions are the real sins, and thoughts should be stopped before they become actions.

[d] Leviticus 19:17 says:

"YOU SHOULD NOT HATE ANOTHER PERSON IN YOUR HEART; RATHER YOU SHOULD TELL HIM WHAT HE IS DOING WRONG. YOU MUST NOT SIN BECAUSE OF ANOTHER PERSON."

In the Talmud, *Arukhim* 16b, the rabbis unpack this verse. They teach (1) that the Torah says "IN YOUR HEART" to show you that the hate, not just the hitting back, is a sin. (2) The Torah makes the connection to TELL HIM to show that it is the actions, not the person, that we want to stop, and we have an obligation to try to help him become a better person. That means we have to try more than once to share with him the error of his action. The last part of the verse, YOU MUST NOT SIN BECAUSE OF ANOTHER PERSON teaches us that sometimes we just have to walk away after we have tried everything else. That is the hard path the Torah wants David to follow.

[20] Is Squealing a Mitzvah?

Three twelve-year-old boys were seen shoplifting some candy from a local store near the synagogue just before Hebrew school. The owner of the store, upset by the repeated robbery of his goods, walked into the synagogue and found the principal's office. Together they walked through the halls and found Simon, one of the boys he recognized. When confronted, Simon confessed to the crime, returned the candy that was still in his pocket and agreed to take whatever punishment would be dished out. On the other hand, he refused to "squeal" on his two partners. The principal told Simon that revealing the names of the other two thieves was the right thing to do. Simon disagreed, saying that while he would take the punishment that he deserved, it was not honorable to get anyone else in trouble.

MAKE A CHOICE: *Decide whether Simon or the principal is right—if caught, should you turn in your partners in crime?*

The Answer to "Is Squealing a Mitzvah?"

Does a thief have to turn in his partners in crime?

[a] Leviticus 19.16 teaches that you cannot let a neighbor be physically hurt:

DO NOT STAND BY WHILE YOUR NEIGHBOR'S BLOOD IS SHED.

[b] In Deuteronomy 21.1-3 the same lesson is expanded to guarding your neighbor's property.

IF YOU SEE YOUR NEIGHBOR'S OX OR SHEEP LOST, YOU MUST NOT IGNORE IT... YOU MUST DO THE SAME THING FOR ANYTHING THAT IS YOUR NEIGHBOR'S—YOU MUST NOT REMAIN INDIFFERENT.

The Talmud, *Bava Metzia* 30b, makes this clear by saying: "If a person sees flood waters approaching someone else's field, that person must make a barrier or a dam and try to stop them in order to prevent damage to the neighbor's property."

[c] Later legal sources (*Mishneh Torah*, Laws of Robbery 1.13, *Shulhan Arukh, Hoshen Mishpat 426.1, Mappah* on *Hoshen Mishpat* 388.11, etc.) expand this law to require the revealing of information when a neighbor will experience financial loss as well. Jewish law makes it clear that every witness to a crime—even one of the criminals—is obligated to come forward and testify.

[21] How Long is "Til Death Do Us Part"?

This one is sad. Dave and Sarah are a couple who have been married for more than fifty years. They have no children. Dave now has Alzheimer's, which has gotten very serious. He needs around-the-clock nursing care. He is not able to recognize people or remember much. Sarah is scared and confused. She has learned that her medical insurance only covers half of what is needed for Dave's medical care. Sarah is in her seventies and has long since retired from her job as a teacher. She is beginning to use up their savings, which will be gone within two years. She will not have a penny to live on. Her lawyer has told her to divorce Dave and protect herself. If she does that, Dave will be cared for by the insurance and by public funds, but her savings will be safe. She feels like this will be abandoning her husband and breaking her marriage vows. She goes to her rabbi and asks his advice. He is now asking your advice.

SOLVE THIS ONE: *Decide what you think Sarah should do.*

The Answer to "How Long is 'Til Death Do Us Part'?"

Can a wife divorce a husband with Alzheimer's in order to protect the nest egg of money she must live on? A case very much like this appears in *Contemporary Reform Responsa* by Walter Jacobs. In his responsum he teaches:

[a] That Judaism very clearly allows for divorce, based on Deuteronomy 24.1 ff that teaches rules for divorce.

[b] In the *Shulhan Arukh, Even ha-Ezer* 117.1ff, 154.1ff, Joseph Caro rules that a wife is allowed to divorce her husband if (a) disease makes it impossible for him to function as a husband any longer, or (b) he is wasting family assets to the point that she feels her future is endangered.

[c] Maimonides, similarly, in the *Mishneh Torah*, *Hilkhot Ishut* 14.17, says that a spouse may set a limit on what will be spent on his/her partner's medical expenses. BUT

[d] both Maimonides and Caro argue that while such a divorce or limiting of funds is legal by Jewish law, it is not ethical or in keeping with the marriage vows.

[e] Jacobs concludes (after consulting other texts about the obligations of a spouse to care for his/her partner) "The wife is duty bound to care for her husband even though there is no hope of recovery. We should seek alternative ways to help her both now and in the future. The lawyer must look for other ways to protect his client."

[22] The Birthday Gift That Bounced

Aunt Bertha had a hard year. She had to borrow money from almost everyone in the family. She owed maybe $10,000 to various family members. All of a sudden her business picked up, she began to make money again and she began to repay her debt. Then all of a sudden she sent Debbie a check for $250 for her twelfth birthday (where usually family members got $25).

Debbie was concerned. She knew about Aunt Bertha's financial troubles. She called Aunt Bertha to ask if the check had been made out for the right amount. Bertha told her, "I am having the best year, my dear, and I wanted to do something nice for you." Debbie was concerned that Bertha still owed thousands of dollars to members of the family. She asked her father if she should keep the money for the sake of *shalom bayit* (good feelings and peace in the family) or return it and ask her to just give her $25 a year until she could pay everyone back.

YOU BE THE JUDGE: *Decide what you would tell Debbie to do.*

The Answer to "The Birthday Gift That Bounced"

Aunt Bertha owed a lot of money to members of the family and still gave Debbie a too-expensive birthday gift. Should it be returned?

[a] In the Talmud (*Bava Batra* 74a) Rabbi Papa and Rabbi Huna ben Joshua have an argument. Rabbi Papa believes that the repayment of a loan is a mitzvah. Rabbi Huna believed that it is just a legal obligation. While most opinions agree with Rabbi Huna, the bottom line is that (1) anyone who does not pay back a loan is considered wicked, and (2) when no period is stated in loan, one should begin repaying it after thirty days.

[b] Encouraging Aunt Bertha to pay back her loans as quickly as possible is the right thing to do.

[c] However, the Torah is also concerned with human dignity. In the Midrash we are told:

"Every time you embarrass another person, you make God less. Every time you make another person feel smaller, you make God smaller in the world, because people are created in God's image" (*Genesis Rabbah* 24.7).

Therefore, to try to follow both commands Debbie must find a way of refusing the overly large gift without making Aunt Bertha feel bad.

A SECOND OPINION: The information given was that Aunt Bertha had begun paying back her loan. Therefore, there is no reason Debbie should return the gift. As long as Aunt Bertha is paying her loan off, it is no one else's business how she spends her income. Nothing requires her to repay the loan earlier than agreed, and there is no reason she cannot allocate her budget as she sees fit. If none of us were to give gifts until all loans were repaid, few gifts would be given, as most people have outstanding loans to banks for their homes and cars. I am not arguing with Rabbi Huna ben Joshua or Rabbi Papa. Neither opinion deals with Aunt Bertha's situation. She is paying back the loan. Aunt Bertha is performing mitzvot both by repaying the loan and by giving her niece a wonderful gift. She certainly is not wicked, and Debbie would be disrespectful to her aunt in assuming she knew best how her aunt should handle her finances. Where is the mitzvah in that? **Eva-Lynne Leibman**

[23] Mishnah Goes to the Movies—Dante's Peak

In *Dante's Peak* (whether or not you saw it) there is a great ethical dilemma. Grandma lives up on the mountain. She is warned about the volcano erupting and refuses to come down. The adults, knowing the danger, are really frustrated but know that it is too late to go get her. The kids cry and complain, but the adults explain the situation. Then, while the adults are busy doing other necessary things, the twelve-year-old boy and the ten-year-old girl steal Mom's truck and head up the mountain toward the erupting volcano to save Grandma.

SOLVE THIS ONE: *Who did the right thing here: the adults, in refusing to try to rescue her, or the kids, in making their own attempt? What Jewish principles can you state to back your case?*

The Answer to "Mishnah Goes to the Movies—Dante's Peak"

Dante's Peak suggests the question, "Can two kids try to outrun the lava in order to rescue their grandmother?"

[a] Jewish law draws a distinction between *safek sakaneh* (possible danger) and *vadai sakaneh* (certain danger). Maimonides teaches:

"One may risk *safek sakaneh* in order to save another person, but not *vadai sakaneh*" (*Kesef Mishneh*).

[b] This idea is rooted in Leviticus 18.5:

YOU SHALL KEEP MY LAWS AND MY RULES, YOU SHALL ACT ON THEM, *YOU SHALL LIVE BY THEM*.

The idea is that no mitzvah is worth dying for (except for three: not murdering, not sexually assaulting and not committing public adultery).

[c] The problem in the film is that the kids believe that the rescue is possible, the mother and other adults that it is impossible. Normally the adults would win because of the commandment HONOR YOUR FATHER AND MOTHER. However, Rashi on Leviticus 19.2 makes it clear that you need not obey your parents when they ask you to violate the Torah. (Not saving a life when possible would be a Torah violation.)

So it all boils down to how sure the kids are that the life is savable—even though the film might not be as exciting.

[24] Who Is Buried Next to the Grants' Tomb?

George Lane was buried in a Jewish cemetery in Philadelphia. After the burial the local board of rabbis tried to have him dug up and moved elsewhere. The problem was that after the burial the authorities learned that George was an active Messianic Jew who accepted Jesus and who continued that faith up to the moment he died. Before the burial the family had told the cemetery that they were Jewish and had always been Jewish. There were no conversions in the family. They later said, "Our lifestyle is Jewish from beginning to end, but we know that Jesus, Yeshua, is the Messiah. We are just amazed that they made such an issue of it."

DECIDE THIS CASE: *Should George Lane, who spent much of his life trying to get other Jews to accept Jesus as God, be considered a Jew? Should he remain buried in a Jewish cemetery?*

The Answer to "Who Is Buried Next to the Grants' Tomb?"

[a] In the Talmud it teaches: "Even though they sin, they are still called Israel" (*Sanhedrin* 44a). This is understood to mean that no matter what sin a Jew commits (including conversion to another religion), he or she is always still considered to be a Jew. *This is also true of a Jew-by-choice. From the moment of conversion, he or she is now "stuck" being a Jew forever.*

[b] An Israeli secular court ruled: "Anyone born of a Jewish mother who has not converted to another religion is to be considered a Jew for purposes of the Law of Return" (Brother Daniel Case).

[c] The American Reform Movement has decided that "anyone born of a Jewish parent who has been raised in a consistent pattern of Jewish involvement is to be considered a Jew" (CCAR).

By traditional understandings, George Lane is a Jew.

[d] We are also taught in the Talmud: "You do not bury a righteous person next to an evil one" (*Sanhedrin* 47a). Commentaries define an evil person as a (a) murderer, (b) sex offender, or (c) apostate (a Jew who tries to convert Jews to other religions).

NOTE: The commentaries on *Gittin* 61a make it clear that Christians may not be buried in a Jewish cemetery. When Jews and non-Jews share a communal cemetery a wall must be built between a Jew and a non-Jew. In a Conservative responsum Rabbi Ben Zion Bergman argues with Moshe Feinstein (Orthodox) that the non-Jewish spouses of a Jew can be buried in a Jewish cemetery. Feinstein says no, even ruling that Conservative converts should be treated as non-Jews. Bergman, while not authorizing the burial of non-Jewish family members by Conservative rabbis, says that a Conservative Jew need not object to burial by Reform rabbis. Bergman argues, "It is wrong to consider a person who supported the Jewish community and raised Jewish children to be evil."

If George Lane had not already been buried, his burial in a Jewish cemetery would be forbidden under traditional Jewish law because he would be considered an apostate, and that would define him as evil. However, Jewish law also (a) forbids the embarrassment of a living person and (b) demands that the bodies of the dead be treated with respect. In this case, the final rabbinic decision was to build a wall one brick high around the grave of George Lane to inform the family that this was not a precedent for the burial of additional Messianic Jews. They also forbid the use of Christian symbols on the headstone.

[25] Does Shabbat Have to Go to the Dogs?

Junior forgot to feed the dog. Mother forgot to back him up. Just as all the company—more than twenty people—was sitting down to the *Erev Shabbat* meal before his bar mitzvah, Kelev Tov, their dog, began yelping and howling and demanding to be fed. Junior said, "Whoops, I forgot to feed him." Mom said, "In all the confusion I forgot to remind you." Uncle Brad said, "Lock him outside and you can feed him after we eat." Aunt Gertie said, "That would be cruel. Lock him outside and feed him after we do the blessings." Cousin David (who was only fifteen and had spiked hair) said, "Wrong! Feed him now. The blessings can wait."

YOU ARE NOW THE RABBI: *What should Junior do?*

The Answer to "Does Shabbat Have to Go to the Dogs?"

Junior forgot to feed the dog. Should the dog be fed before the meal begins? Or after the blessings? Or after the meal?

[a] I think the dog should be fed. In Judaism there is a law that you can't be mean to animals. The dog doesn't know what the blessings are. He'll probably think he is being punished when he didn't do anything. **Alyssa Levin-Scherz, Grade 4**

[b] There is a mitzvah called *tzar ba'alei hayyim*. It forbids being cruel to animals. Not feeding is a form of being cruel. In Genesis 24 Rebekkah draws water for all the camels. In Numbers 20 Moses brings water out of the rock for people and for their animals. From these stories the rabbis learned that animals are to be fed before people. Even the wicked Laban did this when he invited the servant into his home.

[c] Maimonides says, "The sages made it a practice to feed their animals before they tasted anything themselves."

[d] The Magen Avraham was a Polish Talmudic commentator, Abraham Abele Ben Hayyim ha-Levi Gombiner. (Some name. That is why he was known by the title of his most famous book, the *Magen Avraham*). In 1692 he argued that it is an absolute obligation, not just a "nice thing," to feed animals first. Rashi, on *Gittin* 70b, says, "One may even delay *ha-Motzi* in order to feed animals."

Cousin David, who said, "Feed him now. The blessings can wait," is probably right. The question that remains is how not to embarrass the elders, Aunt Gertie and Uncle Brad, who had different opinions.

[26] Can "Sludge" Be a Sign of Friendship?

David has ADHD. It was much worse when he was younger. Then he could never sit still and never do anything for very long. Everyone used to say "Dave has ants in pants" and stuff like that. Now that he is fifteen he has learned to control himself better. He has also gotten good at knowing when he needs to take his Ritalin and when he can get away with skipping it. Once, when he was eight or nine, a counselor at day camp said to him sarcastically, "David, think 'Sludge' and just ooze somewhere slowly—just for once." From that day on his nickname at camp was "Sludge." He never liked the name. He was hurt by the name, but he got used to it. All of a sudden, this week, Karen (a girl he really likes) remembered the name and started calling him "Sludge" again. Now a bunch of his old friends have picked it up. None of them even remembers the story of how it started. For them it is an act of love—a pet name. For David it still hurts.

YOU BE THE JUDGE: *You are David's best friend. He shares his feelings with you. What should you do?*

The Answer to "Can 'Sludge' Be a Sign of Friendship?"

When David was eight or nine the other campers used to call him "Sludge." Now, at fifteen, some of his friends have started using it again. They think it is an act of friendship. He thinks it still hurts. What should the one friend to whom David told the whole story do about it?

[a] In the Torah it says:

YOU SHALL NOT CURSE THE DEAF, AND YOU SHALL NOT PLACE A STUMBLING BLOCK BEFORE THE BLIND; YOU SHALL FEAR YOUR GOD — I AM THE ETERNAL

Ramban, Rabbi Moshe ben Nachman, a Sefardic commentator, taught:

"When you put a stumbling block before a blind person he can trip and fall and be hurt. When you curse a deaf person how can she be hurt by words she cannot hear? The answer is easy: Even though she cannot hear the curse, she can still be lessened in the eyes of others and therefore angered or embarrassed by them." If one may not insult a person who cannot hear, it is certainly wrong to hurt someone who is aware of what is being done to him.

According to the rabbis, saying anything that lessens the way other people think of a person is forbidden. An insulting nickname is clearly a violation of this mitzvah.

[b] There is a Bible story you probably did not learn in Hebrew school. In Genesis 9:22 we learn that after the flood Noah gets drunk. His son Ham walks into his tent and then goes outside and tells his brothers about it. The Hofetz Hayyim, a Polish teacher who specialized in studying the use of words, taught:

"Ham committed two sins. First, he failed to cover up for his father and stop him from embarrassing himself. More importantly, because he went outside and told others about Noah's condition, Ham was cursed by God because he failed to protect his father's dignity."

[C] The *Kitzur Shulhan Arukh*, Chapter 63, teaches:

"If a person has an unpleasant nickname, even if s/he has become used to it and is no long embarrassed when it is used, another person should not call him/her by this nickname (if the intention is to embarrass him/her). To do so would be 'wronging with words.'"

This helps—but not completely. The friend should clearly stop using the nickname but has to decide if there is a way of stopping others from using it without further embarrassing David. Causing more embarrassment (by explaining the name) might well be worse.

[27] Stealing Stolen Property from a Thief

Everyone knew that Roger was a thief. He had been caught many times. Judy's video game was missing from her desk. Everyone suspected Roger. Judy went over and asked Roger. He said, "No way!" Even so, Aviva saw it in his desk. She recognized it from the Band-Aid that held the lid over the batteries shut. The week that Judy had bought it she had dropped it, and Aviva had fixed it with a purple Band-Aid with flowers all over it. They got into a big argument over what to do. Aviva wanted Judy to just steal her game back from Roger. Judy said, "Stealing is wrong—even from a thief. I would go and tell Moreh Sarah, our teacher." Sivan heard them talking and said, "Squealing would be wrong, too. The three of us should go to Roger and tell him that we know—and that he has to give it back."

FIGURE IT OUT: *What do you think Judy should do?*

The Answer to "Stealing Stolen Property from a Thief"

Roger probably stole Judy's video game. Can Judy try to steal it back?

[a] In the Torah it says:

YOU SHALL NOT STEAL (Exodus 20.13).

In Leviticus we find the same commandment:

YOU SHALL NOT STEAL, YOU SHALL NOT DEAL FALSELY, AND YOU SHALL NOT LIE TO ONE ANOTHER: YOU SHALL NOT SWEAR FALSELY BY MY NAME, THEREBY DESECRATING THE NAME OF YOUR GOD — I AM THE ETERNAL (Leviticus 19.11-12).

[b] The rabbis wanted to know why this commandment was repeated. In the *Sifra*, a midrash on Leviticus, Ben BagBag explains that the Leviticus version of this mitzvah means,

"Do not even steal back from a thief that which s/he has stolen from you, so that you will not appear to be a thief yourself."

Ben BagBag learned this from the rest of the verse, which is all about deceit. It is DEALING FALSELY even if it is not actually stealing. It is meant to keep society from becoming a mess, with people stealing and stealing back.

[c] A little bit further on in Leviticus 19 it says:

(1) YOU MUST NOT HATE YOUR BROTHER OR SISTER IN YOUR HEART. (2) YOU MUST CERTAINLY REBUKE YOUR NEIGHBOR. (*"Rebuke" is giving them negative feedback that could help them.*) (3) AND NOT CARRY A SIN BECAUSE OF THEM (Lev. 19.17).

The rabbis were interested in the arrangement of this verse, with three mitzvot jammed into one sentence.

Rabbi Samson Raphael Hirsch explained the connection between (1) and (2): "YOU SHALL NOT HATE... IN YOUR HEART. The verse speaks of your enemy as your brother. Even though he wronged you, think of him as a brother and do not fall prey to hatred."

The *Sifra* explained the connection between (2) and (3): AND DO NOT BEAR A SIN BECAUSE OF HIM. It is a mitzvah to rebuke someone who has wronged you—but if you do it the wrong way, you will be sinning. Be careful not to embarrass the person.

In this case the rabbis want you to confront the thief and perform the mitzvah of *tokhekhah* (rebuke), or if that will not work, they want you to use the courts—in this case, the teachers.

[28] Hallel On Yom ha-Atzmaut

Hallel is a series of psalms that are said on religious holidays. They are said on the three festivals: Sukkot, Pesah, and Shavuot. Hallel is not said on Shabbat, Rosh ha-Shanah or Yom Kippur. But Hallel is said on Hanukkah. Hanukkah is a holiday when miracles took place and the Jewish people were saved. When the State of Israel was created, some Jews started saying Hallel on Yom ha-Atzma'ut, Israeli Independence Day. Other Jews said "No way. Yom ha-Atzma'ut is an important day, but the modern state of Israel is no miracle." In legal literature there is a big argument, with different rabbis going different ways.

IF THE DECISION WAS UP TO YOU: *Would your synagogue say Hallel on Yom Ha-Atzmaut this year? What is your thinking?*

The Answer to "Hallel on Yom ha-Atzmaut"

Here is the perfect example of the way that halakhah works. Here are two different, opposite answers to the same question.

Rabbi Ralph Pelcovitz argues: "The Talmud makes it clear that Hallel is to be said on days when miracles occurred, on days 'whenever Jewish communities are delivered from imminent danger.'"

[a] Here is that text: Rabbi Yohanan said in the name of Rabbi Simeon ben Yehozadak: "In Israel there are eighteen days on which an individual says Hallel. They are the eight days of Sukkot, the eight days of Hanukkah, the first day of Passover and Shavuot, the Festival days of the Feast of Weeks."

Outside of Israel one says Hallel on twenty-one days: the nine days of the Sukkot, the eight days of Hanukkah, the two first days of Passover, and the two days of Shavuot.

Why don't we say Hallel on Purim when a miracle also happened? Said Rabbi Isaac: "We don't do it on Purim because no Hallel is said for a miracle that occurred outside the Land of Israel."

Rabbi Nahman ben Isaac disagreed. The Exodus from Egypt is a miracle that happened outside the Land, he said, and yet we say Hallel on Passover. Easy: Before Israel entered the Land of Israel, all the lands were considered sites for Hallel-saying miracles; once Israel entered the Land of Israel, no other countries were considered to be the source of miracles that could trigger Hallel (*Arakhim* 10a).

[b] Based on this text, Rabbi Pelcovitz concluded: "It can be argued that in 1948 and in 1967... such was the case...and it is proper to thank God for our salvation." He adds, "The question of saying a *brakhah* over this Hallel is more complicated."

[c] Rabbi Moshe Tzvi Neriah argues that the declaration of a modern State of Israel does not represent an acknowledged miracle, and it had significance only for a limited portion of the Jews and not the whole nation. He concludes, "Only with a rededication to the study of Torah—that happened with Hanukkah—can the recitation of Hallel have significance."

[d] Rabbi Meshulam Roth read *Pesa<u>h</u>im* 117a and concluded that we are empowered to declare Yom ha-Aztmaut a time for Hallel.

Rav Judah quoted Samuel: "Hallel was sung by Moses and Israel when they exited from the Red Sea. And who ordered this Hallel? The prophets among them ordained that Israel should recite it at every important victory... and when they are redeemed they recite it in gratitude for their redemption."

Rabbi Roth argued that the establishment of the state was a victory that required Hallel.

[e] Rabbi Aaron Soloveichik compromises and says: "The saying of Hallel will become an obligation only when it affects the entire Jewish nation—and this will happen in the days of the Messiah. The establishment of the State of Israel affected the lives of Jews all over the world—but it affected them only as twelve million individuals and not as a single community. When the Messiah comes Israel will be a single community—and then Hallel with a blessing will be an obligation. May we merit that day soon."

These four Orthodox rabbis have two different opinions—
WHOSE SIDE ARE YOU ON?

[29] A Chip Off the Old Tooth

This is a real case from an anonymous sender. The chairman of the school board wrote:

"Recently one of the students in the Hebrew school was roughhousing and pushed another boy's head into the table, chipping his tooth. We were trying to think of some Jewish consequence for the boy. Do you have any ideas? Some project or task or ???"

When I asked questions to get more information I learned:

"The offender was ten years old, an Aleph student. It was not mutual. The offender just decided for personal reasons to take the action. He did not intend to cause the harm rendered, and we do not know what his real intention was. Obviously it was one of those events that happens when you are fooling around instead of practicing the four questions, as you are supposed to. The offender is known to the principal—i.e., he had been sent to the office before. He did not really have a history of violence, though."

IF THIS CASE WAS BROUGHT TO YOU: *How would you sentence the ten-year-old?*

The Answer to "A Chip Off the Old Tooth"

One ten-year-old attacked another and chipped his tooth. The school asked advice as to a "Jewish solution." I wrote and suggested three things.

[a] The Torah says (Exodus 21:23-5):

YOU SHALL AWARD A LIFE FOR A LIFE; AN EYE FOR AN EYE, A TOOTH FOR A TOOTH, A HAND FOR A HAND, A FOOT FOR A FOOT; A BURN FOR A BURN, A WOUND FOR A WOUND, A BRUISE FOR A BRUISE.

Rashi explains: "If one person blinds the eye of another, that person has to pay the value of his eye.... In the same way all other cases are to be dealt with, but it does not mean the actual cutting off of the offender's limb, as our rabbis have explained in *Bava Kamma* 83b."

The "tooth for a tooth" parallel from Exodus screams out. Rashi makes it clear that "tooth for a tooth" means financial responsibility. Therefore the boy should pay to fix the tooth.

[b] The obligation to do *t'shuvah,* to offer a real, heartfelt apology is also clear. This must be sincere and not just a show.

If a person has transgressed any of the mitzvot in the Torah, on purpose or by accident, he or she must confess before God, repent and turn away from sin (Maimonides, *Laws of Repentence*, 1.1).

Perfect *t'shuvah* (repentance) is where a person has the chance to repeat an offence and refrains from doing it because of the repentance and not because of fear of punishment (Maimonides, *Laws of Repentence*, 2.1).

Repentance on Yom Kippur only atones for sins committed against God. For sins committed against another person, even if one has paid back any loss, one must go to the injured party and ask forgiveness (Maimonides, *Laws of Repentence*, 1.9).

[c] He must do *heshbon ha-nefesh*, the right kind of spiritual work so that change (and the purging of anger) can take place.

Akabya ben Mahalalel said: "One who heartfully asks four things will never sin again. Where do I come from? Where am I going? What am I destined to become? Who will be my judge?" (*Avot d'Rabbi Natan*, 19).

The Actual Solution: The principal met with the boy and his family. The boy provided a written apology to the teacher and to the boy who was hurt. The offender, on his own, volunteered to pay for the chipped tooth repair out of his allowance.

[30] A Twelve-Year-Old's Right to Die

Bennie, a twelve-year-old in Florida, has a kidney transplant. His body begins to reject the kidney, so the doctors dramatically increase the dosage of the anti-rejection medicine. The medicine makes the boy sleepy. It blurs his vision. It makes it hard for him to concentrate. He can't really read, watch television or play video games. Even visiting with friends is hard, because his eyes become very light sensitive. He and his mother decide he should go off the medicine and take his chances. He says, "Living this way is not living." The doctors call it "suicide" and "parental abandonment of responsibility." Bennie and his mother argue that it is his life. The doctors go to court. The court orders the family to continue medical treatment. You are part of a Jewish team advising the court on medical ethics. You speak for the Jewish tradition.

Question: *Can a twelve-year-old (with his mother's permission) make a decision to reject the medical treatment that will keep him alive? Should he?*

The Answer to "A Twelve-Year-Old's Right to Die"

This Talmudic story is the core of Jewish thinking about treatment of the dying.

[a] When Rabbi Yehuda ha-Nasi was dying the rabbis ruled that everyone must fast and pray for God's mercy. They also made it a rule that anyone who said "The rabbi is already dead" would be put to death as a murderer. Then the rabbi's servant woman went onto the roof of his house and prayed, "The angels and people are in a war. The angels are praying for the rabbi to come and join them. The people are praying for rabbi to remain with them. Prayers are fighting prayers. God, may it be Your will that that the human prayers defeat the angels' wishes."

Later, when the servant woman saw how much the rabbi was suffering, she prayed again. This time she said, "May it be Your will, God, that the angels win." Rabbi suffered more and more but stayed alive. The servant woman picked up a jar and threw it off the roof. It hit the ground and made a big smashing sound. The rabbis stopped praying for just an instant. In that instant the soul of Rabbi Yehuda ha-Nasi departed for its eternal rest (*Ketuvot 104a*).

Based on this story in the Talmud, later rabbis concluded that Jewish law teaches that while we can allow someone to die (and stop keeping him alive) we can do nothing to hasten his death. While it may seem to contradict the story, Jewish law teaches that while we need not put a person on a respirator, once the machine has been started, it cannot be taken away.

[b] Rabbinic thinking leans to the view that the patient *should* undergo a procedure if the choice exists. Nevertheless, he may exercise the option to do nothing.

A central factor to be considered is the track record of the treatment. The less sure the doctors are of the possibility of cure, the greater is the patient's prerogative to not have the procedure. In those cases where the doctors are not confident of the outcome, one can choose to live whatever amount of time he has left and not take a chance on losing even that short time, or he can take a chance that he will lose everything—but might gain a lot.

Rav Moshe Feinstein has taught a number of times in his responsa that a patient has a right to refuse treatment and that a person is not required to undergo treatment that will cure his illness but force

him into a life of pain. He teaches that the decision is really in the hands of the patient, who is entitled to know all the options and make his own decision.

Even against the patient's express will, however, he must be provided with food and oxygen. However, we must act upon a request for a stopping of further medical treatment, even if this will bring a quicker death (Rabbi Alfred Cohen).

Jewish medical ethics would encourage Bennie to go back to his treatment but accept his decision to refuse the medication.

[31] Potato-Peel Matzah

Just before Passover 5702 (1942), a group of Jews working in the kitchen at Kovno ghetto managed to steal a bunch of potato peels. They had almost no wheat flour from which matzah could be made. But by mixing the wheat with the potato flour, there would be enough flour to make matzah. The problem was that in order to use these peelings they would need to be washed. When the wet peels were mixed with flour there was a risk of the flour leavening and making the matzah *ḫametz* (not fit for Passover). Without the potatoes there would not be enough flour for matzah. With it, the matzah would not be kosher. Big problem.

AS A FAMILY DECIDE: *What should the Jews of Kovno do?*

The Answer to "Potato-Peel Matzah"

In 1942 Jews in the Kovno ghetto were short on flour to make matzah. They were going to grind potato peels down and make potato flour to mix with the kosher wheat flour. The problem was that in order to be used they had to be washed. Washing them threatened to make them *hametz* and therefore not fit for Passover. There is no prohibition against potato peels being wet—they are not *hametz* and can't become *hametz* no matter what is done to them. If these washed peels were mixed with wheat, the wheat could become *hametz* from being wet.

[a] The rabbis of Bergen-Belsen wrote this prayer for Jews who needed to eat *hametz* on Passover.

> Our Father in heaven, it is known and revealed before You that it is our will to do Your will and to observe the festival of Passover through the eating of matzah and by not violating the prohibition of *hametz*. For this our hearts are grieved—that our enslavement prevents us and we are in danger of our lives.... Therefore it is our prayer to You that You keep us alive and preserve us and redeem us speedily so that we may observe Your statutes and do Your will and serve You with a perfect heart. Amen.

[b] Rabbi Abraham Shapira ruled that they could not wash the potato peels but could wipe them with dry cloths and then mix the dry peelings with flour to make matzah. As long as water was not added to the mixture it would still be kosher.

[C] Here is a parallel case. Just before Passover 5703 (1943) the Nazis delivered a two-week shipment of bread to the ghetto. Jews are not allowed to eat bread during Passover, and during Passover they are not allowed to own any bread. Usually Jews sell their *ẖametz* to non-Jews and then buy it back later if they want to have it after Passover. That was not possible in the ghetto. Rabbi Ephraim Oshry made it possible for Jews to keep bread rations given out during Passover to eat after Passover by arguing that the rations belonged the Nazis and not to the individual Jew. He also stressed that this was a matter of life and death—because they were getting too little food anyway—which transcends most other issues of Jewish law.

It is interesting that in the face of the Holocaust, Jews did not just do the easy thing and ignore the tradition; they still honored God and the Torah by finding legal work-arounds.

[32] Two Much Vacation Is Too Much

Nina (twelve) and Yoni (almost fifteen) have parents who are divorced. Their parents "time share." Weekdays are with Mom. Weekends are with Dad. And vacations are divided. Usually the parents are good at dividing up the vacations evenly, but the last part of summer vacation after camp is a problem. Mom wants to go to England with the kids to visit some old family friends. Dad wants to take the kids on an Alaskan cruise that will include mountain climbing, kayaking, and helicopter rides over glaciers. Either vacation would be great. The problem is the folks want to take these vacations at the same time—and have left it up to the kids to choose which family vacation they want. The kids ask your advice. How do they chose between a vacation with their mother and a vacation with their father?

NOW IT IS YOUR PROBLEM: *What advice would you give?*

The Answer to "Two Much Vacation Is Too Much"

Nina (twelve) and Yoni (almost fifteen) have parents who are divorced. Their parents "time share." Mom wants to vacation in England with the kids. Dad wants to take the kids on an Alaskan cruise. How do they chose between a vacation with their mother and a vacation with their father?

[a] One of the Ten Commandments reads:

HONOR YOUR FATHER AND YOUR MOTHER, THAT YOUR DAYS MAY BE LONG IN THE LAND THAT THE ETERNAL, YOUR GOD, GIVES YOU (Exodus 20:12).

EACH ONE OF YOU SHALL RESPECT HIS/HER MOTHER AND HIS/HER FATHER (Leviticus 19:3).

Rashi, the medieval Biblical commentator, points out that one of the commands begins "FATHER AND MOTHER" and the other begins "MOTHER AND FATHER" to make sure that your parents are equally regarded.

[b] In the Talmud, *Kiddushin 31a,* we have a case similar to our vacation problem.

The son of a certain widow asked Rabbi Eliezer, "What do I do when my father says 'Give me water' and my mother says 'Give me water' at the same time? Who comes first?"

The answer in the Talmud, hard to directly apply today in most families, is that the father should be served first, since "the wife is also required to provide for her husband's needs."

[c] The *Shulhan Arukh* (*Yoreh Deah* 240:14) considers the same case but states that the parents are divorced. Here the suggestion is that it is the child's choice which of parents to serve first.

[d] The Maharshal, a sisteenth-century Polish *posek,* Rabbi Shlomo Luria, argued that it is wrong for the child to choose which parent to honor. What he or she should do is bring one glass of water and place it on the table between them, in essence saying, "You work it out" (*Yam shel Shlomo, Kiddushin* 1:62).

Applied to our case, the kids should tell their parents, "It is wrong for kids to chose between parents—you work it out."

This case was drawn from "The Challenge of Honoring Parents in Contemporary Social Conditions," Rabbi Shmuel Singer, *The Journal of Halacha and Contemporary Society*, Fall 1987.

[33] The Fast-Food Find

Debbie is spending her summer vacation on roller skates. She is not at the rink. She is not practicing her dancing. She is not doing double axles. Instead she skates over to cars and asks: "Do you want fries with that?" She is a waitress at a newly created 1950's drive-in. One day in the parking lot she finds a gold coin purse with $280 in it. She turns it in to Lost and Found. It stays there for a month. After a month she asks if anyone has claimed the purse. The owner tells her, "You can keep the purse if you want, but I am taking the money." Debbie says, "But I found it." The owner says, "But you found it in my parking lot while I was paying you to say 'Do you want fries with that?'" Because they both belong to the same synagogue, they go to the rabbi to solve the conflict. The rabbi asks your help.

SOLVE IT: *Decide who should keep the purse and the $280.*

The Answer to “The Fast-Food Find

Debbie finds a gold coin purse in the parking lot with $280 in it. She turns it in to Lost and Found. After a month she asks if anyone has claimed the purse. She and the owner argue as to who should keep the money.

[a] Both Daniel Ludmir and Lorraine Rosenblatt wrote to us suggesting that the found money should be given to tzedakah. While the money may be given to tzedakah, Jewish law does not require that it be given away.

In the Mishnah, *Bava Metziah* 2.2, we learn:

“If you find one of the following things you must try to return them: Money in a purse, an empty purse, a pile of money.”

In the previous mishnah, *Bava Metziah* 2.2, we learn:

“The following found objects may just be kept: scattered money, small sheaves of grain in public areas, loaves of baker’s bread.”

Based on this text we learn that once we attempt to find the person who lost the purse and the money, it can be kept. It need not be given to tzedakah.

[b] In Mishnah 6 of the same chapter we learn that after a reasonable amount of time trying to find the owner, the finder can keep what is found. Mishnah 4 talks about a find in a store. It says if the find is behind the counter, the store owner keeps it; if it is in front of the counter (like in the parking lot), the finder keeps the find.

[c] In the Gemara, *Bava Metzia* 12a, we learn that if someone works for a wage for another person, she or he may keep what he or she finds on the job, unless collecting finds is part of the job.

The bottom line: Debbie can keep the money and the purse.

[34] Using the Benefits of Nazi Science

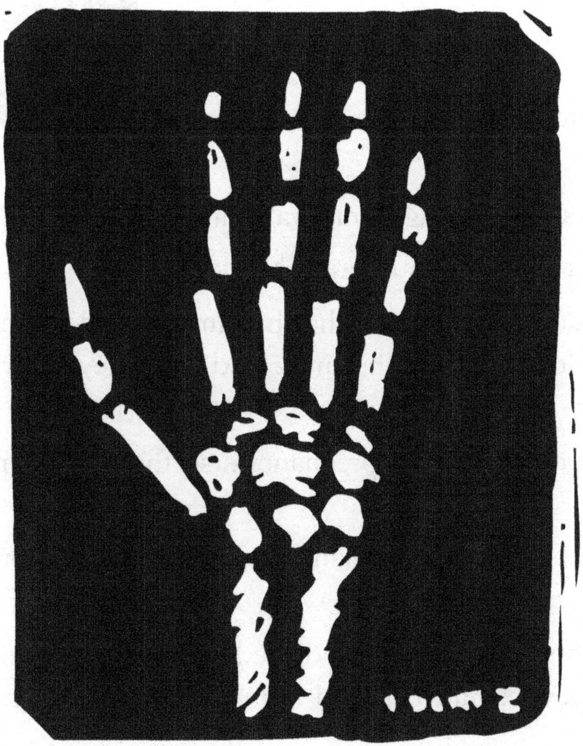

During the Holocaust, Nazi doctors immersed subjects in near-freezing water to see how long the people lived. They died. The experiment was repeated over and over. Hundreds of people were killed, the scientist was branded a murderer, but the work was meticulously detailed and was published. Twenty-five years later, during the Vietnam war, U.S. pilots were shot down over the Indochina Sea. The Air Force needed to know how long to search for pilots and when to give up. To save money and save lives the search and rescue team commander unhesitatingly reached for a book with data from the Nazi experiments.

YOU BE THE JUDGE: *Should this book be destroyed? Can one use information gained by unjust means, even when of critical benefit? Won't this data encourage others to conduct similar gruesome experiments?*

The Answer to "Using the Benefits of Nazi Science"

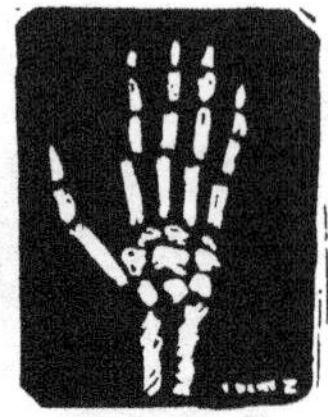

Can scientists today use the findings of Nazi scientists? We specifically used the case of Dr. Sigmund Rascher, who froze more than three hundred Jews to death to learn about hypothermia. This information was used by U.S. Air Force doctors during the Vietnam war to figure out how long to search for downed pilots.

The Talmud has two cases where medical science is advanced through immoral deaths.

[a] Cleopatra's experimentation on the wombs of servants she murdered (Niddah 30b).

A story is told that Cleopatra, the queen of Alexandria, sentenced her handmaids to death by royal decree. They were subjected to a test, and it was found that both a male and a female embryo were fully fashioned on the forty-first day.

Rashi: "They were impregnated and killed at various points in their pregnancies so that Cleopatra could understand the development inside the womb."

[b] Rabbi Ishmael's students learning the number of bones in a human body from a woman put to death by the king (*Bekhorot* 45a).

Rabbi Judah quoted Samuel: "The disciples of Rabbi Ishmael once dissected the body of a prostitute who had been condemned to be burnt by the king. They examined it and found two hundred and fifty-two joints and limbs."

[c] Rabbi Baruch Cohen investigated this question in the *Journal of Halacha and Contemporary Society*, Spring 1990. He concluded that complete censorship of this data would be foolish when human lives can be saved. But, quoting Robert J. Lifton, he adds, "this data should only be used when it also fully exposes the evil things the Nazis did. "

[d] Lord Immanuel Jakobovitz, former Chief Rabbi of Great Britain, also concludes: "Using this data in no way gives meaning to the deaths that created it—and it would be wrong to suggest that they died for a purpose."

[35] The Synagogue's Big Score

The Kleinmans often wind up arguing about local issues at the dining room table. This week the big fight was all about the synagogue lottery. Each ticket was $100. The big prize was $10,000. Barbara, the mother, argued that it was wrong for a synagogue to use gambling to raise money. Gambling can become an addiction. Gambling can cause people to waste needed money. Gambling is just the wrong thing for a synagogue to do. David, the husband, said, "It is just a once-a-year fund-raising gimmick. You're making too big a deal out of this. After all, some synagogues run a bingo game every week." Stephen, age nine, said, "$10,000—cool. What is our chance of wining?" Patty, age twelve, said, "People should just give money to the synagogue; they shouldn't need a prize to do the right thing." The Kleinman family vote wound up in a tie.

IF YOU WERE THE RABBI, *would you allow the synagogue to earn money through gambling?*

The Answer to "The Synagogue's Big Score"

The Kleinman family argued about the synagogue lottery. This argument has been going on a long time. While there is no clear ruling in rabbinic law, there is a strong opinion.

[a] Louis Jacobs (an Orthodox rabbi from England) wrote:

"While gambling in a mild form is not forbidden in Jewish law, it is hardly an ideal occupation... for the devout Jew."

[b] The Committee on Jewish Laws and Standards of the Conservative movement wrote:

"We urge all the members of the Rabbinical Assembly to be alert to the evils of gambling...and the unwholesome consequences of gambling as a mainstay of synagogue fiscal management."

[c] Walter Jacob concluded his Reform responsum on the same question by saying:

The Jewish tradition has found it impossible to prohibit gambling...it would be wrong to make such funds the basis for synagogue life. We urge synagogues to refrain from using gambling as a way of raising funds on a regular basis."

That is as close as we can come to an answer.

[36] Can an Already-Returned Bicycle Be Stolen?

Sam and Judith are next door neighbors. They both are bicycle racers. Once, when Judith's bicycle was broken, she asked Sam if she could borrow one of his. Sam came in seventeenth in that bike race; Judith came in third. After the race Sam said to her, "If you ever need to borrow a winning bicycle again, just ask me." Today, the morning of the race, Judith's bike broke again. She went to ask Sam, but he was already gone. She went in the side door of his garage and borrowed his second-best bike without permission. This time she won the race. Her picture was in the paper. The bike had already been returned when Sam saw the picture in the paper and called her a thief. She said, "A borrower," but he said, "You are a thief."

SOLVE THIS DISPUTE: *Decide who is right.*

The Answer to "Can an Already-Returned Bicycle Be Stolen?"

Judith borrowed Sam's second best bike without permission and won the race. After her picture was in the paper and the bike had already been returned, Sam called her a thief.

[a] Maimonides says (Laws of Theft 1:3):

"If a person wants to borrow a tool and the owner is not around, and it will be put back before the owner returns, is it permissible?

"If it had been borrowed before and one knows that the owner would not be angry, then it would be permitted. If the owner would mind, it would be stealing. "

[b] In our case, the owner seems to have minded, so it was wrong. "I'm sorry. Next time I will ask" should solve the situation.

[37] Pink Boxers

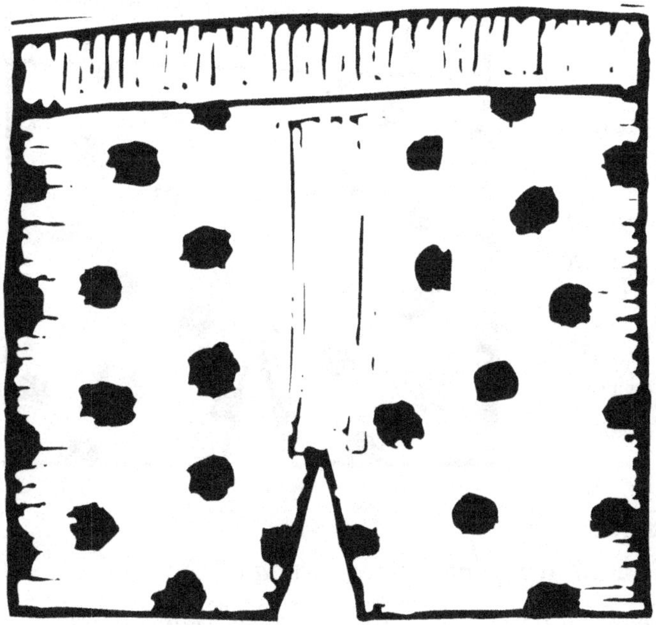

David was in college. He rented a room from Mrs. Schwartz. The two of them worked out a deal. David would schlep his laundry and her laundry to the laundromat and back. Mrs. Schwartz would do all the laundry. David thought it was great, almost the deal that he and his father had during high school. That afternoon David picked up a bag that had been left for him on the back porch. He only made a few stops along the way. The rain didn't bother him that much. And because the laundry was going to be washed, it didn't matter if it got soaked. It didn't matter except that Mrs. Schwartz had packed the colored things on top, and they bled down into her whites. She tried bleaching out everything she could, but some things were ruined. She said, "David should pay for the ruined clothes because he was careless." David said, "She didn't warn me that there was a need to be careful. I am sorry, but it is not my fault."

IT'S JUDGMENT TIME: *Figure out who should pay and why.*

The Answer to "Pink Boxers"

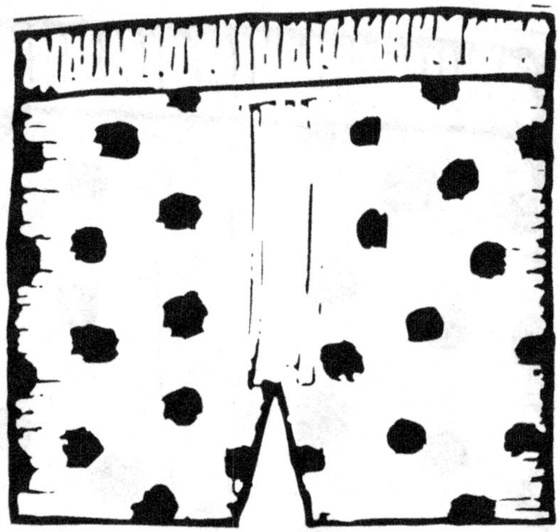

David picked up a bag that had been left for him on the back porch. It rained, but because the laundry was going to be washed, it didn't matter if it got soaked. It didn't matter except that Mrs. Schwartz had packed the colored things on top, and they bled down into her whites.

[a] Rabbi Solomon ben Simon Duran once solved a similar case. In his case a man transported wool goods on his donkeys. The dyed goods were on the first donkey, the white goods on the second donkey. When they hit the river the dye spread onto the white goods and ruined them.

Rabbi Duran, the Rashbash, ruled that the donkey driver was responsible because he was entrusted to get the goods to market. When one is entrusted, one is responsible for all negligence (*Bava Metzia* 82b).

[b] Rabbi Meir said: "If a person moved a barrel for a neighbor from one place to another and in doing so broke it, whether he was paid or not he has to replace the barrel unless he takes an oath that the breakage was not a matter of negligence."

R. Judah ruled: "An unpaid person must swear; a paid person is responsible."

When the rain started David should have checked the bag to see what could be ruined. He is responsible.

[38] Do the Pledges of the Father Fall on the Children?

Sol Goldstein was a very famous Holocaust survivor who lived in Chicago. He was the one who organized the 1978 protest against a Nazi march in Skokie. He also made a large pledge to the Jewish United Fund; when he died $666,000 was still unpaid. Now that his children have inherited his estate, they have refused to pay the remainder of the pledge.

The children argue that their father's commitments are not theirs—charitable contributions are matters of the heart. The children agree to give this amount to charity—but not the charity their father chose. The UJF has brought suit, claiming that a charitable pledge is to be regarded as a legally binding contract.

YOU ARE THE COURT: *Must this pledge be paid to the charity of their father's choice?*

The Answer to "Do the Pledges of the Father Fall on the Children?"

When Sol Gordon died, $666,000 of a million-dollar pledge remained unpaid. Rabbi Betzalel Ashekenazi solved such a case.

[a] A husband and wife had an agreement that if she died first, 20,000 dinars would go to their children and 10,000 dinars would go to him. On her deathbed she changed her mind. She still wanted the 20,000 dinars to go to the children and grandchildren, but she now wanted the 10,000 to go to the synagogue. The husband went to a rabbi and asked if she had the right to change the original agreement.

[b] Rabbi Betzalel wrote: "The heirs do not take title while the person making the promise is still alive. The case is indisputable; a will may be changed. The synagogue is entitled to the 10,000 dinars."

By rabbinic law the heirs of Sol Gordon must make good on his pledges.

[c] In a Chicago court it was also found that the heirs of Sol Gordon must make good on their father's pledge because of the expectation created by the pledge. People were hired, rents were paid, programs were begun based on an expectation of three years of funding.

[39] Priceless at Twice the Price

Zelda and her mother love garage sales. They are very good at finding real treasures among the junk. One day they are hunting at a garage sale down the block. It is Dahlia and her mother's garage sale. Zelda and Dahlia are in the same class at school. Zelda and her mother find a vase on sale for seventy-five cents. Zelda's mother knows that it is worth hundreds of dollars because it is a signed piece from an important porcelain designer. The next day at school Zelda tells Dahlia in a nice, not a mean, way what a good buy the vase was. That afternoon Dahlia's mother calls up Zelda's mother and demands the vase back. She says to Zelda, "You cheated me and bought it way too cheaply." Zelda's mother says, "I bought it at the price you asked."

YOUR TURN: *What is fair and just here?*

The Answer to "Priceless at Twice the Price"

Zelda and her mother love garage sales. They find a real treasure among Dahlia's junk. Dahlia's mother complains: "You cheated me and bought it way too cheaply." Zelda's mother says, "I bought it at the price you asked."

In Maimonides, *The Laws of Acquisition,* we learn:

[a] That both a buyer and seller must be honest in transactions. Neither can cheat or defraud the other (12.1).

[b] Making more than a twenty percent profit on something is considered dishonest, and the laws of fraud say that the deal should be canceled or the difference (up to twenty percent) should be repaid (12.4).

[c] These rules of unfair profit apply only to necessities of life, things like food, clothing, etc. When it comes to luxuries, a buyer and seller may charge and pay what they want. (14.2)

Porcelain vases are luxuries, so the deal is legal (if not fair). Zelda's mother can keep the vase (but Zelda may lose a friend).

[40] The Dilemma of Heinz

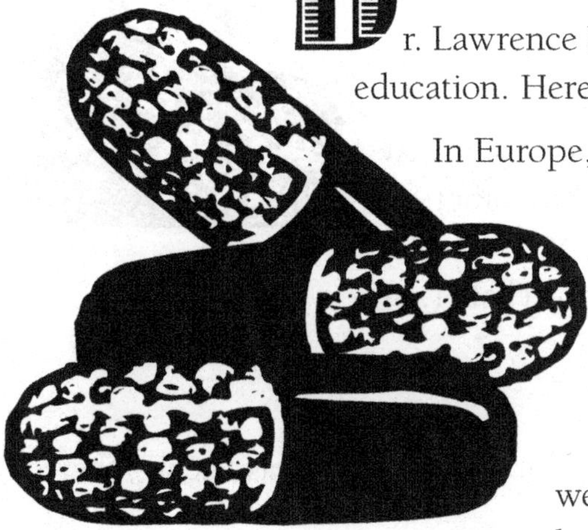

Dr. Lawrence Kohlberg (z"l) pioneered the use of "moral dilemmas" in values education. Here is his most famous case:

In Europe, a woman was near death from a special kind of cancer. There was one drug that the doctors thought might save her. It was a form of radium that a druggist in the same town had recently discovered. The drug was expensive to make, and the druggist was charging ten times what it cost him to make. He paid $400 for the radium and charged $4,000 for a small dose of the drug. The sick woman's husband, Heinz, went to everyone he knew to borrow the money and tried every legal means, but he was only able to raise about $2,000. Heinz asked the druggist to sell it to him cheaper or let him pay later. The druggist said, "No, I discovered the drug, and I'm going to make money from it." So, having tried every legal means, Heinz got desperate and considered breaking into the man's store to steal the drug for his wife.

YOU BE THE JUDGE: *Should Heinz steal the drug?*

The Answer to "The Dilemma of Heinz"

[a] Saving another person's life is an obligation.

Anyone who can save someone else's life and does not do so transgresses: YOU SHALL NOT STAND BY THE BLOOD OF YOUR NEIGHBORS (Lev.19.16). Similarly, if one sees a neighbor drowning in the sea, accosted by robbers, or attacked by wild animals and can save the neighbor personally or can hire others to save the neighbor and does not act, he transgresses YOU SHALL NOT STAND BY THE BLOOD OF YOUR BROTHER (*Sanhedrin* 74a: Maimonides, Laws of Theft 1.14).

[b] However, the cost of saving a life is not always simple.

If X was chasing another, Y, to kill him/her, and Y broke some things while s/he was fleeing, there are two cases:

[1] If they belonged to X, the person fleeing need not pay, because his/her life is more valuable than the broken property.

[2] But if they belong to someone else, then Y must pay, because s/he can't save her/his own life at a neighbor's expense.

If Z was chasing X in order to save Y's life and Z broke something along the way, it does not matter if it belonged to X or Y or another person; Z is not responsible for what is broken. Because if we do not make this rule, no one will try to save a neighbor from a pursuer (*Sanhedrin* 72a).

[c] Rabbi Mark Dratch:

Based on the text in Sanhedrein 74a, Heinz may steal the medicine to save his wife's life, and he need not pay for it or be considered a criminal. He is saving another's life.

[41] A Lime-Green Plastic Skirt with a Bright Orange Angora Wool Sweater

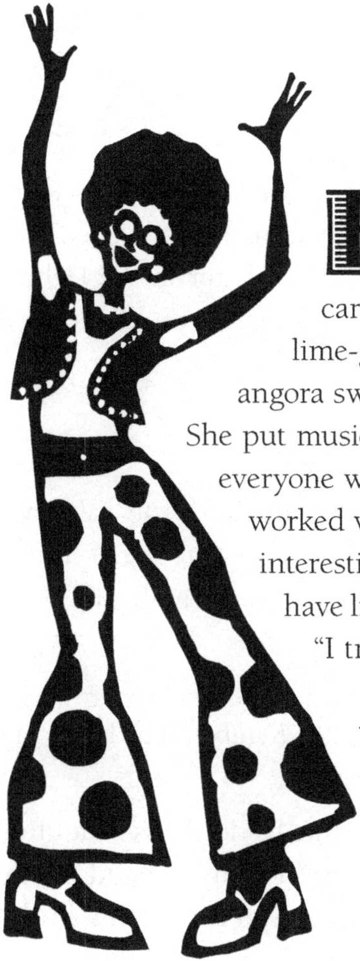

For the first time ever, Carol went shopping with her mother's credit cards. She got to pick out the clothes she wanted. She came home with a lime-green plastic skirt, silver platform sandals, a yellow top, and an orange angora sweater. She went upstairs and got all dressed up—makeup and the works. She put music on her boom box and paraded like a model down the stairs. She asked everyone what they thought. Mom put a smile on her face and said, "You must have worked very hard to put this outfit together. It is lovely, dear." Dad said, "It is very interesting." Carol ran upstairs crying. She shouted, "If you didn't like it, you could have lied." Mother turned to Dad and said, "You should have lied." Dad answered, "I try to never lie."

YOUR TURN: *What should Dad have said?*

The Answer to "A Lime-Green Plastic Skirt with a Bright Orange Angora Wool Sweater"

Carol buys her first outfit on her own. Both of her parents dislike it. Mother tells her it is pretty. Dad says, "It is interesting." Mother tells Dad he should have lied.

[a] In Judaism, truth is really important.

EMET is the Hebrew word for truth. Resh Lakish said: "Tav is the end of the seal of the Holy One." Rabbi H̲anina said: "The seal of the Holy One is EMET." Rabbi Samuel ben Nah̲mani said: "The EMET stands for people who fulfilled the Torah from ALEF to TAV." ALEF is the first letter in the Hebrew Alef-Bet. TAV is the last letter. EMET is made up of ALEF, MEM, and TAV. MEM is the middle letter in the Hebrew Alef-Bet (Shabbat 55a).

[b] Yet there are models for lying.

At the school of Rabbi Ishmael it was taught: Great is the cause of peace, seeing that for its sake even the Holy One told a half-truth. We are told that Sarah said, HOW CAN I HAVE A CHILD WITH AN OLD HUSBAND? (Genesis 18.12). When God retold her words to Abraham, God said that Sarah said, HOW CAN I HAVE A CHILD WHEN I AM SO OLD? (18.13).

[c] But this is the text that is most directly to the point. In the Talmud, *Ketubot 16a*, Hillel and Shammai have the same argument. They discuss telling a bride she is beautiful.

Hillel says, "Every bride is beautiful." Shammai asks, "How can you tell a lame bride she is beautiful?" Hillel says, "Look at it this way. If a man spends a lot of time and money picking out and buying something, it is precious to him. One says to him, 'You have picked perfectly.' So it is with a bride." Hillel wins.

Dad should say something believably nice about the outfit.

[42]: HANUKKAH HANDICAP

This question was once asked of the Maharashal (Rabbi Shlomo Luria, Lublin, Poland, 1510—1573): Should a blind person light a *Hanukkiyah?* What makes this question hard is this: the point of lighting a *Hanukkiyah* is seeing the flames and remembering the miracle. A blind person cannot see the flames.

BE A HALAKHIC SCHOLAR: *What is the right answer to this one?*

The Answer to "Hanukkah Handicap"

The question is whether a blind person should light a Hanukkiyah.

[a] It is not a mitzvah for every person to light his or her own Hanukkah menorah. The Talmud says (*Shabbat* 21b):

"Each household is required to light a Hanukkiyah. Having each person in the family light his own Hanukkah light is an enhancement of the mitzvah."

[b] Based on this, Maharashal wrote:

"If he is part of a family, he should join the family in lighting (with someone else handling the flame.) If he lives with others who are not his family, he should contribute money to the oil or candles but should not do the actual lighting. If he lives alone, he should light his own Hanukkah lights with the help of someone else."

[c] The mitzvah of wearing *tzitzit* is just as important. About them the Torah makes it clear THAT WHEN YOU SEE THEM (Num. 15.39) is the reason we wear them. Still, a blind man is required to wear them. The same should be true of a Hanukkiyah.

TO TALK ABOUT: *Why should a blind person wear a tallit? Why should a blind person have help lighting a Hanukkiyah?*

[43] ONE PERSON'S THEFT IS ANOTHER PERSON'S JOKE

The Kaufman family was one of those that made lots of family rules. They even had a family Bet Din (a family court) where they could bring cases. Most importantly, they had a set of family punishments. If you were cruel to a family member, you had to apologize up to three times or until the injured party accepted your apology. If you stole something that belonged to someone else, you had to pay five times its value. If you ruined something through carelessness, you had to pay twice its value. Family members could negotiate "out-of-court" settlements—but if it went to the judges, these were the rules.

David stayed up all night working on a paper for school. Everyone (especially Mom and Dad) kidded him that it was stupid to always leave his work for the last moment. He printed his paper and then didn't save it to the hard drive. He was done. He didn't even turn the computer off. His younger brother, Matt, got up early and decided to play a joke. He saved the file with the paper onto the hard drive, then removed five pages from the middle of the paper. At breakfast David showed the paper to Mom and Dad. When they noticed the missing pages he went crazy, screaming and throwing things in the air. Then Matt did his "Gotcha." David brought it to the family Bet Din. He said, "This was stealing." Matt said, "It was just a joke. You lost nothing. The most I owe you is an apology." David said, "It was theft—I want payment at minimum wage for five times the ten hours I put in on it."

YOU BE THE JUDGE: *What should be done in this case?*

The Answer to "One Person's Theft is Another Person's Joke"

The Kaufman family has rules. If you are mean, you must apologize. If you ruin something, you must pay double for it. If you stole something, you must pay five times its value. David worked all night on a paper. Matt stole part of it as a joke. He later returned it. David is demanding the "theft" penalty. Matt confesses to being "mean."

In his collection of *Laws of Theft*, Maimonides teaches a lot of key values.

[a] Anyone who steals property worth a penny or more trangresses the commandment: YOU SHALL NOT STEAL (Exodus 20.15) (1.1).

[b] It is forbidden to steal the smallest amount. It is likewise forbidden to steal in jest, or to steal with the intention of returning the object without paying for it. All this is forbidden because one may become addicted to it (1.2).

[c] Who is a thief? One who takes another person's property secretly without the owner's knowledge.

[d] Remember this story from the Midrash about small thefts:

"In Noah's time, when someone took a bushel of beans to sell in the marketplace, another person would just walk by and grab less than a penny's worth of beans to munch on. The muncher didn't worry about it, because all he took was a couple of beans. Then another person would do the same thing. And then another. Soon the bushel was empty. There was nothing left to sell! There was also no one to take to court to make pay. This is how chaos destroyed the world" (*Genesis Rabbah* 30).

[e] In Leviticus 25.17 we find another law:

DO NOT HARASS ONE ANOTHER—HAVE FEAR OF YOUR GOD.

Rashi explains: "This means do not cause each other grief (especially with words). One should not annoy another or give bad advice. Do not pretend that you can say, 'It was the best advice I could give' when you know it isn't. Remember to FEAR GOD, because God knows what is really in your heart. God knows what you were planning, even if you can fool others and yourself."

Even if Matt gets off the hook for stealing (which he actually did do), he is in violation of this last command.

[44] Home Alone for Purim

This case was brought to Rabbi Yechezkel Katzenellenbogen, who lived and taught in Atlona, Germany, in the late sixteenth and early seventeenth century. He was told there was a small town with only ten Jewish men in the general area. This community had a custom of forming a minyan only on Yom Kippur and Purim. Otherwise people celebrated and prayed at home. One year for Purim one of the ten decided to stay at home and not bother coming into the town for the minyan. He said he would read the Megillah on his own—and that others could do so, too. Without a minyan the Megillah could not be read in public.

YOUR VERDICT: *Can the community force this man to attend? What can they do?*

The Answer to "Home Alone for Purim"

[a] In the Mishnah we learn:

"It takes a minyan of ten to pray the Shema and her blessings out loud, to pray the Amidah aloud, to have the blessings of the priests, to publicly read Torah" (Megillah 23b).

The Gemara then adds the reading of the Megillah to the list.

[b] Rabbi Yechezkel Katzenellenbogen ruled that while reading the Megillah at home fulfills one mitzvah, staying at home negates the obligation "to proclaim the miracle of Purim" which requires a minyan. Denying that command is a violation of Jewish law. He ruled that while the holdout cannot be excommunicated, he could be sentenced to receive lashes. (In those days, Jewish courts had teeth.)

[c] The Marashal and the Rema (two other legal commentators) ruled that a fine should replace the lashes. In other words, the man should be forced.

[d] There is, however, another solution. In the Talmud we find:

Rabbi Yehoshua ben Levi also said: "Women are under the obligation to read the Megillah since they also profited by the miracle of the Purim story" (*Megillah* 23a).

[e] While most Orthodox rabbis disagree with this statement, Rabbaneu Nissim, the Ran, wrote: "Women can help men fulfill the obligation of hearing the Megillah, because it is their obligation, too. They can be counted in a minyan for this purpose" (Commentary on Megillah 23a).

The other solution here is to follow the reading of the Ran and count the women in this minyan.

[45] An Unhappy Wedding

Ben is ten years old, and Devin, his brother, is twelve. Crystal has been their babysitter for almost four years. Now she is getting married. They are happy for her, but unhappy that she invited them to the wedding. On one thing they agree, "Weddings are boring." They know for sure that weddings are boring, even though they have never been to one. They figure that a wedding is just like a regular service with a longer *Oneg Shabbat*. They say, "We are not going." Mom and Dad say, "You two are going." Then they find out that Ben's final soccer game of the season—the regional championship—is at the same time as the wedding. He says, "You can't make me miss that for some chance to wear a tie." They say, "You will look good in a tie, dear, and besides, you need practice wearing one." Eventually the dispute goes to a higher authority. You have been brought in to make this decision.

MAKE A DECISION: *Do Ben and Devin have to go to Crystal's wedding?*

The Answer to "An Unhappy Wedding"

Crystal is getting married. Ben and Devin are trying to get out of attending her wedding. Ben has a soccer championship. Devin just thinks it will be boring. Do they have to go?

[a] It is a mitzvah to rejoice with the bride and groom and make them merry (*Brakhot* 6b, *Shulhan Arukh*, EH 65,1, *Mishneh Torah*, *Hilkhot Avel* 14,1).

[b] This is a rabbinic mitzvah, not a biblical one, although it is sometimes included in YOU SHALL LOVE YOUR NEIGHBOR AS YOURSELF (Leviticus 19). The bottom line is this: One should participate in a wedding unless there is a hardship that would be involved in participating. Even if one doesn't participate, one is still obligated to celebrate with the bride and groom.

[c] If the parents need to, they can pull out the big gun: HONOR YOUR FATHER AND MOTHER.

The rabbis expand this mitzvah to include:

A son must not stand in his father's place nor sit in his place, nor contradict his words, nor tip the scales against him... he must give him food and drink, clothe and cover him, lead him in and out (*Kiddushin* 31b).

Based on these words, he doesn't get to say no to most reasonable parental orders.

What happened was this: Ben's team lost, and Devin had a great time at the party. Devin told Ben, "You made the wrong choice, sucker!"

[46] To Fast or Not to Fast

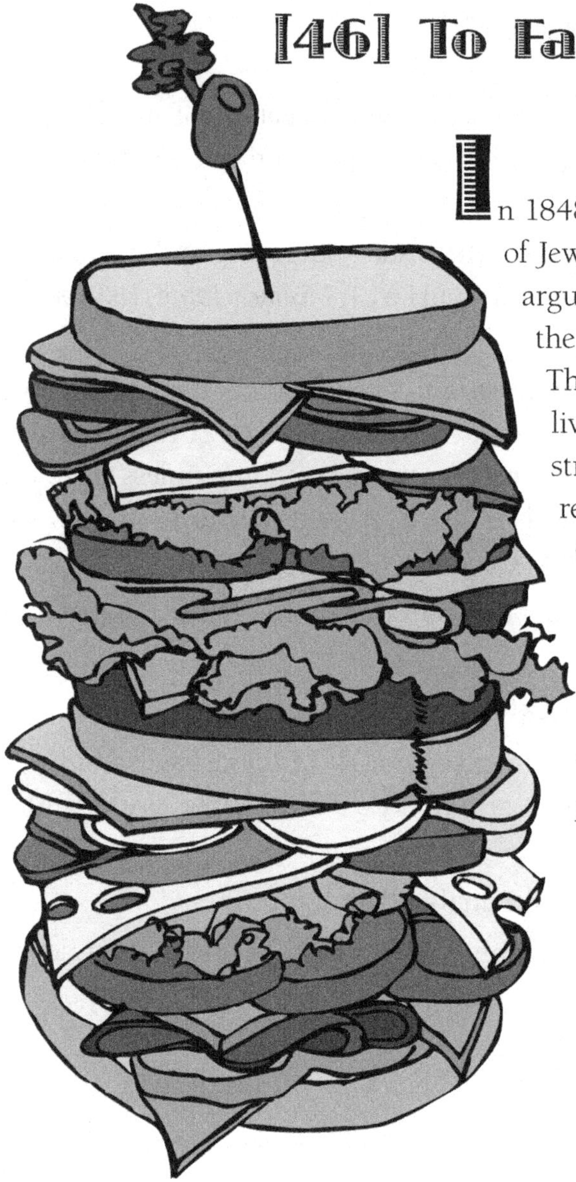

In 1848 there was a big cholera epidemic in Vilna, Poland. Lots of Jews were dying. Yom Kippur was approaching. Some Jews argued that no Jew should fast on this Yom Kippur because the lack of food might make people tend to get sick faster. They argued that this year, skipping the fast would save lives. Their argument was that they needed physical strength. Another group of Jews argued that fasting and repenting was the only way to save lives. They said that God was the only thing that could keep them safe and heal them. They decided that they needed spiritual strength.

IF YOU WERE IN VILNA THAT YEAR:

Would you have eaten or would you have fasted on Yom Kippur? How would you decide?

The Answer to "To Fast or Not to Fast"

Rabbi Israel Salanter faced this real problem. He had to consider a number of texts.

[a] Maimonides teaches that fasting on Yom Kippur is a major mitzvah:

"A positive mitzvah concerning Yom Kippur is that we are required to abstain from eating and drinking on that day. This is taught in Leviticus 19.28, YOU SHALL AFFLICT YOURSELF. Our tradition explains that 'AFFLICT' means 'fasting.' If a person fasts on Yom Kippur, s/he fulfills a positive mitzvah; if a person eats or drinks, he both breaks a positive mitzvah and violates a negative mitzvah, as it is taught in Leviticus 23.29: ONE WHO WILL NOT FAST ON THAT DAY WILL BE CUT OFF" (Yom Kippur 1.4).

[b] However, he also teaches:

"The Shabbat is overruled whenever danger to life is involved, just as we do with all other mitzvot. Therefore, we may attend to the needs of a sick person who is in danger as prescribed by the physicians, and we may violate, on his behalf, even one hundred Shabbatot, so long as he stands in need and is in danger, or if the matter is in any doubt.

"It is forbidden to delay, in any way, violating the Shabbat in order to help the dangerously ill, as it says in Leviticus 18:5, AND HE SHALL LIVE BY THEM. *This means a person shall live by the mitzvot and should not die from observing them.* You see the laws of Torah do not breathe vengeance, but rather mercy, loving kindness, and peace" (Shabbat 2.3).

[c] On the eve of Yom Kippur Israel Salanter appeared on the bimah and publicly ate—urging all of the Jewish community not to fast that year.

Do you think he did the right thing?

[47] Camping with the Enemy

Zev came from a traditional family. They kept kosher. They observed Shabbat. They walked to synagogue every Saturday morning and never ever went shopping or watched television before three stars were in the sky on Saturday night. Zev lived in a neighborhood where everyone lived the same kind of Jewish life his family did. Zev went to a Jewish day school where everyone understood Judaism in the same way. One weekend Zev was supposed to go to camp with all different kinds of Jews—Jews who were as traditional as his family and Jews who were a lot less traditional. They were going to have lots of discussions. Zev didn't know what to say. He believed that any Jew who did not follow the rules of the Torah was doing the wrong thing. He also did not want to be rude or get people angry during the weekend.

BE A GOOD JUDGE: *Talk about what Zev should say or not say during this weekend.*

The Answer to "Camping with the Enemy"

Zev was going to a weekend with all kinds of Jews. Should he tell other Jewish kids that his understanding of the Torah is right and that their Jewish lives are wrong?

Maimonides makes this one difficult (for a halakhic solution).

[a] First he tells us that it is a mitzvah for a Jew to love every other Jew (*Hilkhot Avel* 14.1).

[b] Then he tells us that we should not love Jews who break the Torah, but rather hate them if they reject our rebuke (telling them that they are doing wrong) (*Hilkhot Deot* 6.1). In other words, it would seem that if Maimonides went to the camp, he would have the need to tell every Jew who did not live a traditional Jewish life that he or she was wrong and should change. If the person did not change, it would seem right to hate him or her.

[c] However, in *Hilkhot Mamrim* 3.3, Maimonides says that Karaites (a group of Jews who reject most of Jewish law) should not be hated, because they were raised by their parents and never had a chance to know correct Judaism. He says, "You should try attracting them to the ways of Torah by peaceful means."

[d] Rabbi Avraham Sherman teaches that this is the way observant Jews should relate to non-observant Jews.

How can you both invite and criticize another person at the same time?

[48] The Case of the Cat That Came Back and Wouldn't Go Away

Jessica has always wanted a cat. Her parents have always said no. Both sides had very good reasons. One day Jessica found a cat on the street. It had a collar—a kind-of-new flea collar—but no tags. She brought it home and fed it. It decided to stay. Her parents said, "You may keep it only until we find the owner." Jessica put up signs everywhere. She took an ad in the local newspaper. She asked everyone. No one knew anything about this cat. A month went by. Her parents said, "Time is up. We've kept the cat you call Mindy as long as we can. Now we have to give her away." Jessica said, "We promised to keep her until her owner was found." Her parents said, "We are never going to find the owner. Time is up."

FIGURE IT OUT: *Who is right? What should happen to Mindy?*

The Answer to "The Case of the Cat That Came Back and Wouldn't Go Away"

Jessica finds a cat she names Mindy. Her parents tell her that she can keep that cat until she finds the owner. After a month, no owner is found. Can the cat be given away?

This case is answered by a single Mishnah.

The Mishnah, *Bava Metzia* 2.7, says:

If someone finds an animal that cannot work to pay for its food, that animal can be sold and the money given to the original owner if he or she is later found.

The idea of the Mishnah is that one need not lose a significant amount of money (more than the value of the object) to return something. From the standpoint of the issues of lost and found, Mindy can be sold or given away.

[49] The Case of "Say it Ain't So, Joe!"

Uncle Charlie is in the hospital. He is old and pretty sick. Joe has been left to take care of his equally old dog Kel (short for Kelev). Joe does a good job of walking and petting, feeding and playing with Kel, but he gets sick, too. Everyone thinks he misses Uncle Charlie too much. Joe has a big problem. He doesn't know what to do. When Uncle Charlie asks about Kel, should Joe tell the truth, or should he lie? His father says, "You always have to tell the truth." His mother says, "Charlie isn't strong enough to hear the truth right now."

JUDGMENT TIME: *What should Joe do?*

The Answer to "The Case of "'Say it Ain't So, Joe!'"

Should Joe tell very sick Uncle Charlie that his dog is also very sick?

[a] The Talmud, *Shabbat 128b*, says that breaking Shabbat and lighting a lamp for a sick blind woman is allowed because knowing that those taking care of her can see might make her feel more comfortable.

[b] Talmud also teaches us, *Moed Katan 23b*, that it is wrong to give a patient a sense of hopelessness.

[c] Rabbi J. David Bleich concludes his study of this question by teaching that telling the truth to a sick patient depends on the patient. Sometimes the patient should be spared. Sometimes the patient will get worse if the truth is discovered.

The answer here is knowing Uncle Charlie and using good judgment.

[50] A Shocking Shabbat

In 1974 a big wind knocked down a bunch of power lines in Jerusalem. The wire was live and carried a lot of current. If someone touched one of the lines, he or she would probably die. On Saturday morning many Jerusalemites would be leaving their homes in order to go to shul or to soccer games. They would be visiting family and friends—all the things that people do on Shabbat. At the power company a big argument commenced. Some people said that the power lines had to be fixed during Shabbat in order to keep people safe. Other people said that the power lines could not be fixed until after Shabbat.

YOU ARE THE JUDGE: *Decide what should be done.*

The Answer to "A Shocking Shabbat"

[a] In the Talmud, *Yoma* 85b, we learn that the rabbis once kindled a fire on Shabbat to save Hillel's life. Hillel had been frozen on a roof all night. They taught, "Better to break one Shabbat so that he can live to observe many Shabbatot." The basic rule is then taught, "*pikuah nefesh* (saving a life) is good enough reason for breaking Shabbat.

[b] When the power cable actually went down Rabbi Joshua Neuwirth argued, "Fix it right away—make sure everyone is safe."

[c] Rabbi Pinhas Epstein argued, "Have guards stand until the end of Shabbat, keeping people safe until then. Then fix it."

FOLLOW-UP QUESTION: *Which rabbi would you follow?*

[51] Are Those the Breaks?

Max bought a brand new BB gun. He and "the folks" had gone through all the rules about what he could shoot at and what he could not. He had agreed that living things were out of bounds. No birds. No squirrels. No snakes—unless someone was in danger. That left almost nothing. He spent a week safely knocking cans off a wall. Now he was bored. He went into the garage and found a really old set of dishes. No one even remembered where they came from. He set up the dishes and had lots of fun breaking plates safely. Mom came out and yelled at him. She agreed that he was following all the rules but added a new one: "You can't break useful things." He said, "That's ridiculous. I should be able to break anything no one in the family wants anymore." Mom argued, "Somebody might want them someday." Max said, "They are ours—we can do with them what we want."

RESOLVE THIS DISPUTE: *Discuss who is right.*

The Answer to "Are Those the Breaks?"

Max bought a brand new BB gun. He set up some old dishes and had lots of fun breaking plates safely. Mom came out and yelled at him. She agreed that he was following all the rules but added a new one: "You can't break useful things." In this case, Mom is totally right.

[a] In the Torah it says:

YOU MAY NOT CUT DOWN FRUIT TREES WHEN YOU LAY SIEGE TO A CITY (Deut. 20.19-20).

[b] In the Talmud that becomes a law called *Ba'al Tashhit*:

"It is forbidden to destroy vessels or garments, or tear down buildings or clog up wells, or waste food in a destructive manner" (*Kiddushin* 32a).

[c] The *Shulhan Arukh* makes this even clearer. It says,

"You cannot waste anything which other people will find useful" (*Laws of Body and Soul*, 14).

[52] Talmudic Television: An ER Moment

On *ER*, a seventeen-year-old cystic fibrosis patient, a boy, is near the end of his life. He wants to die in peace. He wants to have a DNR order placed. There is no question that he will die soon. He wants to die peacefully. His mother (and his sister) can't live with his decision. So when the doctor allows him to die peacefully, according to his wishes, they order him to restart his heart and insert a breathing tube. By American law, the child is still a minor, and the doctor has to follow the mother's wishes.

SOLVE ONE LAST CASE: *(1) What do you think is the "right thing" for the doctor to do (if there weren't a law)? And (2) What do you think Jewish law would say?*

The Answer to "Talmudic Television: An ER Moment"

Can a seventeen-year-old's request for a DNR order be honored when his mother demands that he be kept alive as long as possible?

[a] We already know from Case 30: "*A Twelve-Year-Old's Right to Die*" that a dying person can ask for a DNR order under Jewish law (CF. *The death of Rabbi Judah, Ketubot 104a*).

[b] Also, under Jewish law, the commandment HONOR YOUR FATHER AND MOTHER applies at any age, so the question of whether a seventeen-year-old is an adult doesn't matter here.

In the *Shulhan Arukh, Yoreh De'ah 241.25* says that you can disobey your mother over choices of schooling and marriage (major life issues). When to die probably falls under this category.

[c] Also, the Rashi to Leviticus 19.2 makes it clear that you need not follow your parents' wishes when they violate the Torah. Based on the Seven Laws of Noah (*Sanhedrin* 56a) causing an animal to suffer *tzar ba'alei hayyim* is a biblical prohibition.

The mother's wishes here are probably wrong and need not be followed.

Made in the USA
Monee, IL
26 August 2026

61208460R00070